rebel with a cause

rebel with a cause

roots, records and revolutions

darcus beese

with David Matthews

NINE
EIGHT
BOOKS

NINE
EIGHT
BOOKS
NEB 029

First published in the UK in 2024 by Nine Eight Books
An imprint of Black & White Publishing Group
A Bonnier Books UK company
4th Floor, Victoria House, Bloomsbury Square, London, WC1B 4DA
Owned by Bonnier Books, Sveavägen 56, Stockholm, Sweden

@nineeightbooks

@nineeightbooks

Hardback ISBN: 978-1-7887-0609-4
eBook ISBN: 978-1-7887-0610-0
Audio ISBN: 978-1-7887-0611-7

A CIP catalogue record for this book is available from the British Library.

Publishing director: Pete Selby
Editor: James Lilford

Cover design by Alex Kirby
Typeset by IDSUK (Data Connection) Ltd
Printed and bound in Great Britain by Clays Ltd, Elcograf S.p.A

1 3 5 7 9 10 8 6 4 2

Every reasonable effort has been made to trace copyright-holders of material reproduced in this book. If any have been inadvertently overlooked, the publisher would be glad to hear from them.

Nine Eight Books is an imprint of Bonnier Books UK
www.bonnierbooks.co.uk

MIX
Paper | Supporting
responsible forestry
FSC® C018072

I don't care if Saturday falls on a Sunday.

– Darcus Howe

Contents

Foreword

Preparing to write this short tribute, I was reminded of an occasion some years ago, a period in time when politicians sought to enhance their street credibility by openly courting the company of music industry luminaries. Following one such encounter, Darcus reported that he had met the Prime Minister. His father, somewhat exasperated, responded: 'No Darcus, you have not met the Prime Minister, the Prime Minister has met you.' It resonated with me at the time. It was a succinct reminder that, in this particular encounter, Darcus was the one of sufficient merit and worth and that it was the PM who was the fortunate one rather than the reverse. It was a reminder too of the extent to which we, as black people, routinely downgrade our individual and collective experiences.

All this is explored within the pages of *Rebel With a Cause* – a truly remarkable insight into Darcus's personal and professional journey over the past thirty years, navigating to the top of the music industry, its lows, huge highs, lessons learned and lessons taught. It is related with both gravitas and visceral honesty, and I am certain it will rightly be regarded as a vital exposition of the ongoing black experience in a white world both here in the United Kingdom and in the United States.

As Darcus's mother, it is an absolute privilege to be invited to write this short tribute and I want to conclude with the following extract, which is for me an important statement of his values:

> What matters is how people perceive and remember you after interactions. Do they view you with respect? ... It all boils down to what one desires from professional and personal relationships. If the goal is to merely be perceived as a good human being, what does that entail? It's almost impossible to always embody that ideal but at the very least, one should strive to be decent and genuine.

I am so very proud to be his mother.

Barbara Beese
March 2024

1

Once in a Lifetime

And you may find yourself in another part of the world
And you may find yourself behind the wheel of a large
  automobile
And you may find yourself in a beautiful house, with a
  beautiful wife
And you may ask yourself, 'Well, how did I get here?'
                                          – Talking Heads[1]

It was like I'd got COVID of the soul.

Just as people could lose their sense of taste and smell from coronavirus, I'd lost my mojo. Every beat, every melody and every lyric I'd ever listened to now had no flavour, no funk, no nothing. I felt numb. What was once euphoric was now just white noise, which for someone running one of the world's biggest record labels was nothing short of a catastrophe. And now there

---

[1] David Byrne, Brian Eno, Chris Frantz, Jerry Harrison and Tina Weymouth; Sire Records Company.

was this. Another black man killed by the police on the streets of my adopted home. Sure, I could disconnect if I wanted to. I could think, *what's it got to do with me? I didn't know the brotha*. I could buy into the media deflections, the political distractions, the 'I feel your pain' denials and just accept that the fella was asking for it. With my Upper West Side apartment, my Caribbean holidays, my industry awards, my this, my that, I could've simply dropped the shoulder on this one, moved on and gone about my business.

I could have. But I didn't.

As I stood in the middle of Union Square surveying the mass of masked protestors with their mashed-up placards, raised fists and voices fuelled with frustration, anger and, yes, hate, I'd seen enough to know things would soon get ugly. Surrounding the square, what was earlier a thin blue line of overweight beat cops overseeing a peaceful demonstration had suddenly turned into a thick, dark mulch of baton-wielding riot police, poised and ready for trouble. 'Let's get out of here,' I said to my wife, Alison, and my son, Darcus Jr. We'd done as much as we could. Having grown up in the Black British civil rights movement and been dragged out on demos, protests and marches before I could even walk, I knew how to read the runes on the street as much as I knew how to read faces in a boardroom. I didn't need President Donald Trump and his incendiary tweeting to know that 'when the looting starts, the shooting starts'. It was time to bounce.

Just like the thousands in Union Square, and the millions right across America and around the world, Alison, Darcus Jr and I had shouted until our throats were hoarse. 'No peace, no justice.' 'Black lives matter.' 'Enough is enough.' But would there ever be justice? Did Black lives *really* matter? When was enough of anything ever enough? Yes, we'd done as much as we could. But now, the light was fading. Trouble was brewing. Police choppers were hovering overhead. Family aside, that afternoon I had also gathered a small group of colleagues from Island US who, during a morning Zoom, were in floods of tears over what had happened in Minneapolis days earlier and wanted to make a stand as a 'show of unity' and protest against the death of George Perry Floyd Jr – the latest statistic in yet another American war, not on drugs, not on terrorism, but on Black people.

Looking back on that bizarre, 'unprecedented' moment in human history, I wonder how much of the radical, empathic zeal that people displayed when they hit the streets or banged pots and pans together on their balconies was born out of a genuine coming together or because in a locked-down world shorn of hustle and bustle and nightshifts and traffic and clubs and gigs, people simply now had time to care.

Heading away from the demo, I felt the veil being lifted, the rose-tinted glasses coming off. The American Dream, for me at least, was over. I'd be lying if I said I hadn't wanted it to come true. Who wouldn't? But to live the dream you have to buy into the fantasy, which for millions of Americans and foreigners alike, meant either being wasted or deluded. Or occasionally both. Unfolding events, however, had given me a serious reality check. Every time I looked in the mirror or caught my reflection in a window I didn't like what I saw. I'd jog past a storefront, check to the side and there I was: hunched over, gaunt, frazzled. Was that really me? Maybe it was the insomnia, the headaches, the atrophying flesh and bone, the stress. Fuck, was that *really me?*

It was 2 June 2020. While tens of millions of people the world over were basically stuck at home baking banana bread in their pyjamas, hoping, praying, begging for the pandemic to end, God knows how many people were on the streets of America and beyond, railing against the latest police killing of an unarmed black man. As the pandemic bit and we all retreated to our little colonies like human ants, countless New York corporates adopted a 'cameras-on' policy so they could monitor staff working from home. Nevertheless, that afternoon I had rallied the troops from my office, and standing shoulder to shoulder with them on that hill, put them, myself and potentially the label in the firing line as America went up in flames.

Despite widespread global support for the cause, organising staff to go on a Black Lives Matter demo simply wasn't the sort of thing that someone like me, the CEO of Island Records, the label that brought you Bob Marley, U2 and Amy Winehouse, did. In organisational terms, the only thing above me was the board of Universal Music Group (UMG) – the same UMG that was the largest of the so-called 'Big Three' record labels in the US. Followed by Warner Music Group and Sony Music Group, together these companies made up the lion's share of the global recorded music market, with independent labels taking up the rear, albeit with a still significant slice of the pie. As of 2022, two of the three major label groups, Universal and Warner, had sold company shares to Tencent Music Entertainment Group, the music streaming arm of Chinese technology and entertainment mega-giant, Tencent Holdings Ltd.

To give you an idea of who I was dealing with, at the time of writing, Tencent was worth $364.54 billion – making it the world's 22nd most valuable company by market cap. If Tencent were a country, it would be the world's 42nd largest economy; in GDP terms it was ahead of Hong Kong, Colombia, Romania and Chile.

Here I was, an Englishman in New York, running a multimillion-dollar label as part of a multibillion-dollar multinational corporation, while simultaneously breaking lockdown and leading a band of fellow musos onto the streets and into a demonstration organised by Black Lives Matter, a quasi-revolutionary outfit denounced by the President as 'a Marxist group that is not looking for good things for our country'.

But times were a changing.

Far from being worried about one of their top execs winding up on the cover of *Billboard* bloodied and in handcuffs with his face shoved up against the wall, UMG, like many corporations, ran with the 'enough is enough' memo that had seen a slew of companies, brands and artists alike take the protest online by posting black squares on their social media feeds as a mark of solidarity with the movement. Suddenly, everyone was an activist. While Trump fiddled as America burned, corporations sought to get ahead of the curve and distance themselves from a state system that, at best, looked unsympathetic regarding the civil rights struggle, and at worst, seemed actively hostile towards it.

So, UMG had scrambled to form a task force, which aimed to 'devise new initiatives and support marginalised communities in the ongoing fight for equality, justice and inclusion' – a noble cause, which I wholeheartedly supported with my time and energy. Since 2014, when BLM hit the headlines following the deaths in custody of Michael Brown and Eric Garner, companies and brands had fallen over themselves to virtue signal their anti-racist credentials. But for all the 'we stand with you' sloganeering and black squares being posted on Instagram by artists – signed to any major label – where were the protest songs? How many got written, recorded and sold or given away during these increasingly dark days of soul-searching and existential angst?

One minute I was 'an artist-first executive', according to *Music Week*, one of *Billboard*'s top 'Change Agents', and one of only three black people running a major record label. The next I felt like I was rearranging deckchairs on the *Titanic*. I'd had enough. Enough of the racism, enough of being the boss, enough of America and, sadly, enough of Island Records, one of the most iconic labels in the history of pop music, a label I'd dedicated the better part of thirty-two years out of the fifty-two I'd spent on Earth. There was a time when I'd tell anyone who'd listen, 'If you cut me, I bleed Island Records.'

Not anymore.

The *Guardian* had called me 'the tea boy who became the boss', Bono proclaimed I was 'a prince of a man', but one of the greatest compliments I've ever had comes from my late father, the irascible social commentator, writer, broadcaster, political activist and former Black Panther, Darcus Howe. One day, having told him I was being awarded an OBE – the 'Order of the British Empire' – for services to the music industry, I braced myself for a tongue lashing. Even though I desperately sought his approval, I feared that accepting an OBE and all that it stood for would fly in the face of his lifelong struggle for racial equality in Britain. I should've known better.

'Darcus, most people who are awarded OBEs are cunts,' he said in typically colourful fashion. 'You are not a cunt. Go pick up your OBE.'

Here we go.

2

Police and Thieves

Police and thieves in the street (Oh yeah)
Fighting the nation with their guns and ammunition
Police and thieves in the street (Oh yeah)
Scaring the nation with their guns and ammunition

– Junior Murvin[1]

Let's get the biographical housekeeping out of the way.

I was born on 15 December 1969 in west London to Barbara Beese and Leighton Rhett Radford 'Darcus' Howe. I was, and still am, my mother's only child, and the second eldest of my father's seven children.

Mum was born in Hackney in 1946. Her father was black, and her mother was white, and only fifteen when she had her, so consequently, she was put up for adoption and grew up in the care system without ever knowing her biological parents. Some years ago she managed to get hold of the file that was kept on

---

[1] Junior Murvin and Lee 'Scratch' Perry; Wild Flower/Island Records.

her while in care. A question in her notes poses the question, 'Is she suitable for adoption?' The answer? 'No, she's too Negroid.' Imagine navigating post-war London and trying to forge an identity for yourself when you faced labels like that, along with 'half-caste', 'half-chat' and 'mulatto'. No wonder she went for the Angela Davis power 'fro. I've never had a conversation with her about whether she was politically active in college or if it was through her relationship with Dad that she realised the fullness of her black identity. But, boy, when she found her mojo, there was no stopping the sista.

They say opposites attract and, well, Dad was certainly cut from a very different cloth to Mum. Born in Moruga, Trinidad and Tobago in 1943, his mother, Lucille, was a schoolteacher and his father, Cipriani, was a headmaster and pastor. My grandfather, 'Cip', was a proper, Bible-thumping, old West Indian, something that both rubbed off on and rubbed up Dad. He attended Queen's Royal College, one of the top boys' schools on the island, and was fluent in Latin and a dab hand at reciting Shakespeare. He originally emigrated to the UK in 1961 aiming to study law but became heavily involved in black activism and political campaigning once he'd seen how badly black people were treated in the UK, especially at the hands of the police. Returning to Trinidad in 1969, he turned his hand to journalism and, inspired by his uncle, the celebrated writer, C. L. R. James, Dad decided to combine his reportage with his political activism and return to the UK.

In a sense, C.L.R., who Dad would later lodge with in Brixton, south London, was an unwitting matchmaker. When he arrived back in London, Dad joined the British Black Panther Movement, which, along with his immersion in west London's rapidly expanding West Indian community, was where he got to know Mum.

When I reflect on it, the strength of Mum as a woman, as someone of mixed race, who as a child was called a 'Negroid baby', which meant no one wanted to adopt her, is incredible. She ended up in care, and yet she raised me. It goes without saying that she played an even more significant role in my upbringing than Dad, especially in the day-to-day aspects and in shaping my life and political views.

Mum probably broke even more barriers than Darcus Sr. He came from a country where there was a population like him, in the majority, with a significant Indian population and a small section of white middle class. Mum, on the other hand, grew up in a place where she wasn't wanted. There was a racial divide. Dad rocked up in Britain as a middle-class, educated and confident individual with designs on being a lawyer. He was an outlier in his time because most Caribbean migrants to the UK from that era (what we now collectively call the 'Windrush generation') were working class, with many escaping economic hardships 'back home' only to face further financial, cultural and racial challenges in the UK.

The previous year, 1968, local civil rights activist Frank Crichlow had established the Mangrove restaurant in All Saints Road, Ladbroke Grove as a focal point for the area's black community, which was known colloquially as 'the frontline'. As much as its nickname sounds threatening, as Mum would later tell me, the frontline, for black people at least, was one of those local hubs where people could find out what was happening, get the latest gossip, share stories and experiences, get advice, be it social, relationship, or, of course, legal. As a restaurant and a club, of sorts, the Mangrove was known for serving delicious Caribbean food and playing good music, but essentially, it was a community centre, and in those days, the last thing the establishment wanted was for the community to be 'centred'.

The police would repeatedly raid the Mangrove under the pretext of looking for drugs – but they never found any. During one six-month period, it was raided twelve times. The police had a clear objective: discredit Frank Crichlow, bankrupt the Mangrove, and deny the black community one of the few precious social resources it had at the time.

But Mum had a clear objective, too.

Aged just twenty-four, with eight-month-old me in tow, along with Dad, Frank Critchlow, Rupert Boyce, Rhodan Gordon, Elton Inniss, Altheia Jones-LeCointe, Rothwell Kentish and Godfrey Millett, she was arrested and charged with incitement to riot after violence broke out between the police and demonstrators when around 150 people marched to Notting Hill Police Station to protest against the police targeting the Mangrove. As part of 'the Mangrove Nine', Mum and Dad became folk heroes after the group were acquitted of the most serious charges following a fifty-five-day trial, which became the first judicial acknowledgement of behaviour motivated by racial hatred within the Metropolitan Police. Dad represented himself in court and is credited as having torn the prosecution's case to shreds.

As Mum said, the trial had been 'a defining moment for black people in Britain, because it gave real meaning to Black Power, in the sense that, here we were taking this stand and taking on the establishment and winning, and not through the artifice of or the words of defence barristers, it was actually black people doing it for themselves.'

But looking at my peers who experienced single-parent house-holds, many of their mums didn't have the means or the energy to be at the forefront of the movement. They were more focused on day-to-day survival, like going to the market on Saturdays.

Mum really went through it back in the day. By the time the case got to court, I was just under two years old, and she, Dad and the other seven were staring down the barrel of a possible ten-year sentence. 'I had a very real fear that, had the jury been taken in by the police lies, we would have received punitive and vindictive sentences,' she has said.

While I don't remember the court case, Mum's torment, or Dad's swashbuckling defence, my earliest memory goes back before the trial to when I was around a year old. I'm being put in a cot and tucked up by a Chinese man. For years, I thought maybe I was suffering from false memory syndrome . . . or I'd been smoking too much weed. Who was the mysterious Chinese man? Then one day I mentioned it to Mum.

She laughed. 'We used to have a Chinese lodger in a flat we rented in Oxford Gardens, Ladbroke Grove,' she told me.

I also have an early memory fragment of Mum and I living in another flat, this time in Putney, southwest London. I would have been three. As the property didn't have a fit-ted bathroom, we would bathe in a galvanised tin tub, which was stored under the sink. Those were the days when people would go to public baths to bathe, often only once a week. Britain was stinky bad back in those days. Cots and baths. There's a psychological connection there somewhere, perhaps something to do with returning to the womb? Or maybe not. This is what years of psychotherapy does to you: it turns eve-rything into a metaphor.

So, like act two of *The Wizard of Oz*, everything kicks into full Technicolor memory in 1974 when we move to Tynemouth Street, Sands End, a white working-class enclave of Fulham, west London. Our first summer there, in 1975, Fulham were in the FA Cup final against West Ham United. We had a massive street party with sandwiches, cake, fizzy pop, and Fulham's black and white colours everywhere. There was black and white bunting festooned across the street, and I wore a massive black and white rosette the size of a sunflower and had one of those noisy wooden football rattles.

Back then, both BBC One and ITV – two of only *three* channels in the whole of Britain, remember – would dedicate the entire Saturday of the final to broadcasting hours of build-up to the game, the match itself, then hours more post-match analysis. In between all this televisual gloop there were celebrity interviews, stories about fans travelling halfway around the world to get to the game, televised charity fundraisers – the works. Half of Britain probably tuned into an FA Cup final. It's how and why I fell in love with Fulham.

I grew up in a nuclear family in the J. Robert Oppenheimer atom bomb sense of the word. Something was always blowing up in the Beese household. Life was far from calm from the very beginning. As a young black boy in working-class west London, experiencing never-ending cycles of stress, tension, drama, violence, racism and economic strain were simply more rites of passage growing up. I was in a constant state of fight or flight, whether it was dealing with school, walking through the neighbourhood, playing out in Fulham and Chelsea, or navigating friendships with both white and black peers. That dichotomy was ever-present: if you stuck to a second-generation West Indian peer group, your cultural field of vision was narrowed; but if you hung around with too many white kids, the brothas and sistas would deem you to be a 'Banachek', a Bounty bar or a coconut. Battle lines had been drawn and most people took a side. Most.

I've always seen myself as being black, but in the ebb and flow of British racial politics, one minute I could be 'mixed heritage' because my maternal grandmother was white, and the next I'm a person 'of colour' because of the colour of my skin. Identity politics was thus never far from me because it was a lived experience. You can't help but be preoccupied with race and identity when the society you live in defines your very being by it, eh?

Often, while driving around Ladbroke Grove with Dad and his friends we'd be pulled over by the police and harassed so much so that I thought that's what the police did for a living: just stop black people in cars. Dad once said on camera, 'There was no way police could stop and search me. I used to say, "Fuck off. off."' The truth is, Dad was constantly harassed by the police, being arrested no fewer than six times. On one occasion, he was sentenced to three months in Pentonville for pushing a racist ticket collector and assaulting a passer-by who decided to intervene while wielding their umbrella. It was a trumped-up charge and Dad was released on appeal following an international campaign. The performance poet and musician Linton Kwesi Johnson even wrote a protest song for his campaign called 'Man Free (For Darcus Howe)':

Darcus outta jail
Race Today cannot fail
Darcus outta jail
Di people's will mus' prevail . . .

As difficult as it is to say, Dad had a propensity for violence, and not just in a revolutionary. anti-police manner. Sure, he was no Lenny McLean, but to an impressionable young boy, violence, whether psychological or physical, is violence. Being open about this side of my father is painful to admit, but let's be real: people tend to set their moral compass firmly in the direction of travel they want to go in rather than where their chosen heroes are headed. Tens, hundreds and thousands of people hero-worshipped Dad for the shift he put in on black Britain's civil rights struggle, on the streets, on screen, and in the corridors of power. That can't be taken away from him. But what they saw publicly is not what I saw privately. Often, Mum and Dad would have blazing rows which would turn physical. Generally, there would only be one winner.

My biggest fear was the alcohol coming out. It's still a trigger for me now, stemming from those times as a child when I'd see my father have one too many and lose his shit. It's not that someone having a drink immediately causes problems or that I have an issue with it – after all, I'm no teetotaller – but drinking was a consistent signal during my childhood that shit was about to go down. When Mum and Dad started drinking, I knew things were going to get difficult, without a doubt. It didn't matter where we were, whether indoors or outdoors with a crowd of people, even at events like Carnival, as soon as the drinking began, I knew trouble was on the horizon and that my day and night were going to be a problem.

I despised that feeling back then. It's something I grew up with, and even in later years when Mum and Dad drank around me, it still affected me because I knew the warning signs all too well. It could be a sideways glance, an old Trinidadian saying, a cutting remark, or a song playing from Mum and Dad's record collection that set things off. Either or both of them could be cooking, maybe they'd have friends over, the drinks would be flowing, and then the needle on the gramophone would touch on some tune and like Manchurian candidates they'd switch: they'd get wound up, tempers would fray, and suddenly – BOOM! – it would kick off. An evening or afternoon that started out in the best spirits ended in hell, because of spirits.

Being an observer – and a listener – I clocked from an early age how music, like alcohol, could change the dynamic between people, and within people. Both struck me as extremely powerful because of their mood-altering effects, but also the way they could play tricks on the mind. It's no wonder music has long faced censorship for moral, political or religious reasons, and why everyone from the Taliban to the BBC has sought to ban individual songs or music, period, at some point. The seed of music being powerful juju was planted in me from an early age.

The role of family and the cultural background you come from can significantly shape how emotions are expressed. But so can alcohol. As a kid, I didn't buy the idea of the 'happy drunk'. You're either happy or you're not. Booze doesn't change that. What I saw is people express their feelings, frustrations and alienation when they were under the influence in ways they wouldn't, or couldn't, when they were sober.

On occasions, things would get so volatile, so out of hand, that the police would show up following complaints from the neighbours. They never did anything other than tell my parents to keep it down, even if Mum was in floods of tears and clearly the worse for wear. The police didn't give a shit. Dad would manage to sweet-talk them and they'd go on their merry way. I'd often hear them laughing as they left the flat, exchanging racist 'bants' as they disappeared into the night, no doubt en route to harass some more black folk in the Grove.

Dad was a no-nonsense kind of guy. You couldn't approach him with any foolish, ill-thought-out or banal questions or issues. If you asked him something or tried to engage him in a discussion, it better be legit because, trust me, if there was any bullshittery going on he wouldn't say, 'Oh, really?' He'd say, 'Bwoy, don't ask such a silly question.'

He had this demeanour that was hard to describe. It wasn't passive-aggressive, and he wasn't overtly paternal, but there was something very fatherly about him, albeit in a detached way. I guess you could call it 'classic Caribbean dad'. There's always a sense of distance, or a Victorian notion that children should be seen and not heard. He was pragmatic, stern, rational. In the Caribbean, he's the guy who shows up with his tools when you're in real trouble, maybe to fix a car or build a massive wall. He'd probably then give you a lecture about what went wrong, and drink your rum out. Whatever the problem was, it would be something way beyond your capabilities, but he could fix it, and then illustrate why you couldn't do it. He was that guy.

Dad was also a walking talking contradiction in terms and, like many an intellectual, a rank hypocrite. He ate cognitive dissonance for breakfast, lunch and dinner. He was forever telling me to 'respect your mother' and 'do as you're told' and preaching that 'black is beautiful', right before giving Mum a lick and then taking off into the night. I'd think to myself, *Hang on a minute: you're preaching to me about respect this and honour thy that, and you're carrying on like what, exactly?*

Given the times, Dad was far from unique in terms of his macho heteronormative behaviour. Growing up with such household, cultural and legal dysfunctionality, was it any wonder that many of my generation would go on to become screwed up and confused? The one advantage I had over many of my peers was that being brought up basically as an only child in a one-parent household gave me that little extra time and space to reflect on the chaos and the mayhem, process it, and move on. Many of my peers, competing as they did with three or four siblings in the same house with the same identikit parents: drunken, womanising, gambling, violent, an occasionally present father and a constantly frazzled, overburdened mother, consequently wound up as drunks, drug addicts, in jail, on the social or untimely dead.

Sometimes, I used to think of my parents' relationship, 'If that's love, I don't want it.' But looking back now, I realise that despite all his shortcomings, if it wasn't for Dad, I wouldn't be who I am today. He had many faults, but there were also those moments, those spectacular instances when it balanced out. What one takes away with one hand, they give with the other. Maybe I'm just a forgiving person; I don't know.

Growing up in west London, activism was never far from me. While my mates were dicking around on Saturdays on the streets, I'd often have to put a shift in on demos with Mum and Dad. And it wasn't always a Black Power thing.

During the summer of 1978, I went on a demo with Mum in support of the Bengali community in Tower Hamlets in London's East End, which was protesting over the racist murder of Altab Ali, a 24-year-old leather garment worker, in May of that year. I was eight and a half years old and dressed in a vest and a pair of raggedy flares. Mum and I stood out, as not only were we part of just a handful of black people on the demo, but apart from the activist and writer, Mala Sen, author of the critically acclaimed, *India's Bandit Queen: The True Story of Phoolan Devi*, and a few other sisters, she was one of very few women. On the day, photographer Paul Trevor took an iconic photo of Mum and Mala holding my hands at the front of the demo as it marched down the famous Brick Lane, a photo that has graced many an exhibition, poster and book cover, I'm proud to say.

Another time, I had to go all the way up to Bradford to be on a demonstration with Mum and Dad over George Lindo, a young brotha who had been fitted up by the police in Bradford for a robbery he didn't commit. There's an iconic picture that's often used to illustrate Britain's 1970s black civil rights move-ment of a scrawny-looking seven-year-old me on top of a truck with my brother and Dad; other photos of me from the period generally don't have me posing outside of Butlin's with an ice cream or petting a giraffe at London Zoo. They tend to have me at the front of a 'black people's day of action' with a raised Black Power fist or carrying a placard with something like 'No Peace, No Justice' daubed on it.

Back on the streets of Fulham, there was an open-door policy in place. Regardless of class, colour or creed, kids would play freely in the middle of the road, running in and out of each other's houses, getting up to all sorts. It was a hodgepodge of different families and nationalities. We had a Greek family; then there were the Lawrences, who were a big English family; two Irish brothers, one of whom I think joined the IRA and got arrested; and a guy called Tony, who ran Olympic Cars, a minicab business, from his front room, who had a driver who was a regular extra in *Doctor Who*.

I grew up next door to Alice, an Irish woman, and her Ghanian boyfriend, Joe. Their story was one of those typical romances from the 1960s that resulted from black immigrants coming over to the UK and, when looking for lodgings, being faced with English landlords who wouldn't rent to them. Often, the only ones offering rooms were Jews or Irish women, and the latter occasionally wound up in assignations with their black male lodgers, which, in its own small way, created a subset of multicultural, multi-ethnic Britain. Alice and Joe were a product of this cultural phenomenon.

Joe was a jazz musician who often played into the wee small hours in bars and clubs across London, so every Saturday and Sunday morning he'd shout groggily from his bedroom window, 'Darcus, are you up? Go and get me my papers.' Off I'd trot to fetch his newspapers, and in return he'd teach me how to play rummy.

The local policeman was called PC Paddy, on account of him being Irish. Despite being 'the enemy', he was a nice fella. He would occasionally come to the school to co-organise a London-wide outreach scheme run by the Metropolitan Police called the Panda Club, which was basically a Met PR exercise designed to turn kids into mini police informants. By participating in the Panda Club, i.e. listening to Met propaganda for an hour, I got a certificate and a picture with me and some other kids posing with PC Paddy in the school playground. When I brought these home and showed Mum, she went nuts: here was a picture of her son, the son of not one but two of the Mangrove Nine, grinning his face off in the playground with a copper, the filth, the pigs, the bumba claat Babylon! She was not a happy bunny.

'Darcus, if that *ever* happens again, just excuse yourself from the group. Do you hear me?'

'Yes, Mum.'

Mum had taught me how to deal with the police, not only on the streets but in primary school, too. There was no fifth column about to emerge in the Beese household, trust me.

Fulham, like much of London, was undergoing a transformation. Gentrification was on its way. We were the first generation of kids growing up on that street, and probably one of the last. The sight of jumpers for goalposts, cricket stumps chalked up on front garden walls, and the mayhem of knock down ginger is now a thing of the past.

I'll admit, I was a bit of a street urchin back then. I wouldn't have looked out of place in the *Little Rascals* or the *Double Deckers*. You only knew it was late when the streetlights went off. I'd get up to things then that make me feel hypocritical for telling my own kids off for their nocturnal antics.

The times and the specific location you grow up in of course play a significant role in the experiences you have and your worldview. Different neighbourhoods and areas, such as Brixton, Fulham or Peckham, each have their unique cultural, social and economic characteristics. These factors can influence the interactions and relationships people have, as well as the challenges they face, especially if you're from second-generation immigrant stock. While we shared many similarities, contemporaries who grew up in a different quarter of London to me, let alone the rest of the country, had their own subtle nuances. Second-generation West Indian EastEnders, for instance, were often more likely to have white mates and girlfriends compared with brothas and sistas from 'sarf', who often struck me as being more socially and culturally homogenous, while West Londoners obviously had the monopoly on cool because of our closer proximity to bohemian London! As for North Londoners, well, what happens in north London stays in north London.

In addition to the geographical and experiential context, political and social background also plays a crucial role in shaping our views, right? Growing up with a backdrop of fighting against the system's racism and corruption can have a profound impact on how individuals perceive and respond to various situations. I grew up in a multicultural household. Dad's first wife, Una, is white and English, and their daughters, my sisters, Tamara and Taipha, are mixed race. Mum's mum was white.

Growing up against the backdrop of knowing that white people, in terms of the system, were an issue, having white friends and white people in your family was challenging at times. Generally, it was a non-issue; until it *became* an issue. Sometimes I'd be out on the street with a group of mates and a white kid – one of your white mates in the group – would say something offensive and racist and it would kick off. You just had to have it out, even if the kid was twice the size of you. I just couldn't let that hit slide because of the way I was brought up and the principles Mum and Dad stood for. I used to come out of those situations in a mess, because eight times out of ten I'd get a pasting. But I was prepared to die on that hill because I wasn't just standing up for myself; I was representing my people. White kids never had that burden of expectation.

Walking to school, picking up a newspaper or watching the telly meant facing a barrage of racist images, from seeing 'NF' or 'wogs out' spray painted on walls, to Liverpool legend John Barnes having a banana thrown at him during a game. That was the backdrop, the context of that era. And then it would come to your doorstep. Chelsea fans who drove or were bussed into town for a home game usually parked near the end of our street, on Imperial Road. When Chelsea played at home, especially against West Ham, Millwall or Spurs, that was the time to avoid Fulham Broadway, stay at home and batten down the hatches, because the streets would be a thoroughfare of the most hardened racists in the capital.

As much as I was into football, I wasn't into it enough to deal with the shit that came with actively supporting a club. Despite the fact that many of the London clubs were the first to have black players, there was no way that I was going to a football match in those dark days of football hooliganism. Unlike Fulham, which has always been a family-oriented, local and relatively trouble-free club, if you were black and you supported Chelsea, West Ham or Arsenal, you were up against it the moment you actually went to a match. Ironically, many black kids from London wound up supporting Manchester United or Liverpool because they could, romantically, dissociate those clubs from their lived experience of racism in their city, and just watch football on telly with no grief.

Going to a football match was fraught with implied and actual danger. To be fair, it was something I was starting to face with increasing regularity going to school or taking a trip to the sweet shop. The growing normalisation of abuse. One day I was going to see my half-brother, Rap, who lived nearby on the World's End estate in Chelsea, and decided to take a shortcut through the back streets. As I neared his home, I turned a corner and saw a mob of Chelsea supporters on the other side of the road alighting from a coach. They clocked me immediately. Cue: 'Ooh-ooh-ooh' monkey chants and 'nigger' this and 'black bastard' that. I was just ten or eleven years old. I couldn't even comprehend how big-arse grown men could hate me like that. Swallowing the abuse, by the time I thought I'd got to a safe distance, I threw up two fingers, told them to 'Fuck off!' and legged it. The next thing I hear is, 'Get the black cunt!' and they're after me. I don't know if they ran for 10 or 15 yards just to scare me, but I didn't look back. When you're running, never look over your shoulder – just run! By the time I got to my brother's house I was as white as a Chelsea racist and wide-eyed, with my eyeballs out on stalks and my heart beating out of my chest. That's when I first realised that these racist hooligans actually wanted to hurt black people; they actually wanted to see blood run from my body. As a kid, I'd never been bullied like that before.

Back in the day, everywhere you turned there was racism. I remember hanging out on a local estate with a bunch of mates, some black, most of them white. One of the white kids named Ollie called one of the black kids a nigger.

'You what?' I said, piping up, to which someone told me to 'pipe down'.

'Nah, nah, nah,' I said, turning my attention back to Ollie. 'You wanna fight?

'Yo, Darcus, calm down,' someone said.

'Yeah, I wanna fight!' said Ollie.

'Yeah, well come on, then,' I said.

It was real kids' stuff, proper handbags at ten paces. That was until Ollie said, 'Wait here,' and went home to put on his steel toe cap boots. Within minutes he returned and we got into a proper tear-up. I got rag-dolled, dragged all over the concrete, scratches and welts on my face . . . I got a proper dusting. On the way home, licking my wounds, I ran into three brothas who went to the same school and who were in the same year as Ollie.

'Rah, what happened to you?' they asked, eyeing up my injuries.

I told them what had happened, and they told me not to worry – they'd catch him outside school. The following day, sure enough, the brothas put it on Ollie. I got my revenge. Problem solved.

Another time in school I got into a spat with a white boy over a bastardised song from a TV commercial, which was a racist play on a jingle for the Dutch beer, Oranjeboom. He got up in this Indian kid's face and started singing, 'Oranjeboom, boom, boom, you're a nigger not a coon.' He just kept singing it over and over and over, the little punk.

'Yo, just watch when we catch you outside,' I said to him, squaring up, my heart racing. I wanted to beat the shit out of this kid so badly.

I went around the school telling some of the brothas in my year that we had a little racist on our hands and he needed to catch some heat. See, this white boy had a crew, so I wasn't taking any chances. Soon enough, *every* black kid in the school was looking for this white bwoy and my name had got put up as the vigilante that had whipped everybody into a frenzy. This brewed such a shitstorm that the school even wrote to my parents about it: 'Darcus was involved in yesterday's incident, and he has been issued with a most stern warning as to his future conduct. If there are any acts of threatened violence, actual violence or gang violence on other pupils it will be necessary to ask you to come into the school to discuss the issue.' There was of course no mention of the white kid throwing racial epithets around in the first place, but that comes as no surprise seeing as schools in the 1970s and 1980s were pretty much an extension of an established system that loaded the dice against black kids like me. This isn't to say that I was a junior rabble rouser, mini-Malcolm X or pint-sized mafia 'don' in school. Far from it. I was certainly a follower rather than a leader. I was never one to take the lead, but often I'd be the kid looking the other way as everyone else ran off, and would invariably get caught. Look, I can't say that I had the best upbringing in the world; certainly it wasn't one I'd measure against the norm. Once the childhood war stories came out with my other friends, they'd be like, 'Holy shit, Darcus! How the hell did social services never come round?' or, 'How come the police were never called on you?'

Anyway, that racist kid got dealt with. Problem solved.

And on and on it went. Slur after slur. Conflict after conflict. Fight after fight. While the likes of Mum and Dad were the generals and field marshals strategising against racist Britain on the battlefields of the courts, parliament and public institutions, black kids were like boots on the ground engaged in adolescent urban warfare, clearing schools, youth clubs, dancehalls and shopping precincts one racist at a time.

One afternoon, after standing on that hill yet again, being called 'nigger' for the umpteenth time that week and getting into a brawl with a gang of Irish kids who lived across the road, I ran indoors crying my eyes out. At this point Dad had moved out – or been kicked out – but nevertheless he would often be around.

'What are you crying about?' he said, looking me up and down.

'Some Irish kid from over the road beat me up,' I said, tears streaming down my grubby face. Dad kissed his teeth, grabbed a cricket bat and put it in my hand.

'What are you doing?' Mum shouted.

'Go and deal with him,' Dad snapped back before Mum grabbed the bat from my hand.

Dad kissed his teeth again. 'Bwoy, don't let these white people fuck with you,' he said before going back to whatever it was he was doing. I knew he'd never, ever let me go out onto the street and smash someone, but he had to illustrate the point to me in no uncertain terms: don't let white people fuck with you.

Occasionally, when the costs outweighed the psychological benefits, i.e., when seriously outnumbered or out-gunned, I'd back down, walk away, and take some shit in the process. But on the whole, I couldn't let racial abuse slide. Imagine your mother, sister or daughter having misogynistic slurs thrown at them whenever they went to work, the shops or school. Constantly. Would you expect them to just take that? Would *you* just take that? That's what being called a 'nigger' means to black people. It means disempowerment, humiliation, inferiority. Call me a 'nigger' and we've got a problem, and not because of how it sounds or even what it means but because of what it represents. And before anyone gets their rag on about its prolific use in hip-hop or grime or even among black people, it's not the word that's the problem, it's who uses it, how they're using it, and where they're using it that's the issue. I don't get to call female friends 'bitches' or gay friends 'fags' because I don't have that privilege or cultural copyright that gives me licence to bandy around such epithets. I don't own those words. Likewise, white people don't get to call me 'nigger'.

Once I realised that I couldn't run all the time, that I couldn't turn the other cheek or just walk away, I knew I had to stand and fight. Crucially, I also realised that fighting, in whatever form, wasn't a 'childhood phase' – I was in it for the duration. That's how I was brought up. The fight or 'the struggle' wasn't a sprint, it was a marathon. Consequently, after that, whether it was in school, or whether it was on the street – and I'm not saying that every time I got into trouble was a racist incident – I couldn't walk away; that's not how I was brought up. Nevertheless, race never got in the way of love, something I realised when I first met Alison. I was just eleven years old. She was my first schoolboy crush. I even bought her a Valentine's Day card, but it took years to turn a childhood infatuation into a relationship. We eventually hooked up when, barely in my twenties, I was strolling down the King's Road in Chelsea with a friend when I ran into Alison pushing a stroller. Tucked up inside the buggy was her eighteen-month-old son, Chad, all blond-haired and blue-eyed. I hadn't seen Alison in an age, but to cut a very long story short, things hadn't worked out with Chad's father, so here she was a single mum . . . and a single woman . . . and there was me . . . still love-struck despite the passage of time. At first, we just started hanging out, casually. But then it all clicked, and Alison became my girlfriend, best friend and eventually fiancée and wife, as well as mother to our three children, Chad, Darcey and Darcus.

Once things had gotten serious between Alison and me, I looked upon and looked after Chad as if he were my own kin. However, when we initially got together, my parents did have concerns about me taking on someone else's child, even though I wasn't old enough at the time to understand the paternal responsibilities, or what the long-term consequences of being in a mixed-race relationship would or could be, given the racist nature of life in Britain beyond the capital's boho villages.

People forget how rough London was in the '70s and '80s, and how backward the rest of the country felt for anyone coming from the Big Smoke. You had a major global capital city on its uppers, still coming to terms with the aftermath of the war. All that Churchillian bluster and braggadocio about empire, the legacy of Enoch Powell and his infamous 'rivers of blood', skinhead boot boys, the NF and little Nazis puffing their chests out was a joke. I don't think most white people bought it, but a significant minority did, which was enough to get the right people elected and newspapers sold. Meanwhile, black people had to put up with a litany of abuse on the street and in the corridors of power.

On 2 March 1981, Dad helped organise a 20,000-strong 'Black People's Day of Action' in protest at the handling of the investigation into the New Cross fire, in which thirteen young black people died under highly suspicious circumstances. To date, no one has ever gotten to the bottom of what really happened on the night of 18 January 1981, let alone been held responsible for what many still believe was a premeditated arson attack. Dad called it 'the blaze we cannot forget', but reggae artist Johnny Osbourne captured the sadness, frustration and rage of Britain's black community when he took the day of action slogan '13 Dead, Nothing Said' and cut the eponymously titled record, which was co-produced by one of my all-time favourite bands, Aswad. Yet again, here was a case of black music paying homage to the black struggle through the art of the protest, struggle or liberation song, something that's been a major theme in black music, from the earliest days of the Delta blues right up to the grime music of today. Growing up, aside from hearing songs that directly related to an event such as the New Cross fire or even my dad's arrest, I'd hear it in poetic or abstract fashion, as in Marvin Gaye's paean to the Vietnam War's legacy, 'What's Going On?', or Bob and Marcia's spellbinding cover of Nina Simone's classic civil rights anthem, 'To Be Young, Gifted and Black', to Stevie Wonder's assault on poverty and injustice, 'Living for the City', or Junior Murvin's rage against Babylon, 'Police and Thieves'. Countless other black songs were not only lyrically and musically powerful, but reached audiences of millions of people around the world.

For a kid who felt voiceless and often alone in the world, music became my solace, my inspiration, and brought meaning to all those protests, demos, marches and sit-ins I was taken to and otherwise might have misunderstood or grown up to resent. While other kids were out playing football, I was literally standing on the shoulders of political giants. I'm grateful that, especially with the support of my mum and dad, I've been able to achieve success and make the most of what they fought for. They fought for people like me. But I'm getting ahead of myself.

When you come from a Caribbean background but you're raised in Britain, you have to deal with multiple identities; you must juggle different elements of your character, of yourself, and your understanding of the world. The mainstream, majority population sees you in a particular way through a Eurocentric lens, and conversely, *you* see your surroundings and environment through an Afrocentric lens, albeit one that is heavily influenced by the prevailing culture. Maybe that's just the way life is – a constant battle or navigation of different and conflicting forces. But certainly, the day-to-day minutiae of my upbringing, with all of its contrariness, helped to shape my character. I can be con-tradictory, which is why I think not *everything* can be reconciled.

Many a time I'd be in a car with Dad and his friends, and we'd get stopped by the police, who, chicken shit as they were, would eye up the number and size of the occupants and, if they had an overwhelming advantage, drag them out of the vehicle and give them a kicking. I'd have my little face pressed up against the car door window watching these custodians of the law, who were there to 'police by consent', indulging in what they used to call 'nigger bashing', laughing and joking as they put the boot in. If you couldn't have it on your toes you'd have to take it, because resistance would amount to assaulting a police officer. Once they'd had their kicks, each officer would straighten himself up, dust himself down, and tell us, 'Now fuck off!' To the average white citizen, who had nothing to do with the law other than buying a dog licence or paying a parking fine, the police were genial bobbies on the beat. To the black community, however, they were an army of occupation. I was in the Mangrove when the Notting Hill Carnival riots happened in 1976. Black people had had enough of the police harassing the hell out of us and arresting us on the trumped-up, illusory charge of 'being black and having a good time in public'.

From a young age, all black people understand – instinctively, experientially and culturally – that music isn't just about partying, socialising, filling uncomfortable silences across a dinner table and making a racket – aurally or financially. We understand that black music isn't just the cornerstone of the blues, the DNA of rock 'n' roll, the progenitor of pop music, and a multi-billion-dollar industry that's become the soundtrack to hundreds of millions of people's lives the world over. We understand that music isn't simply noise. Why? Because when you come from a culture where listening to music gets you arrested, where playing it gets your records banned, your equipment confiscated and you thrown in jail, and where singing and making videos of it can get you killed, you realise that music is defiance, defiance is freedom, and freedom, ultimately, is power.

In the Beese–Howe household, as in *all* Caribbean homes of the day, music wasn't just about pleasure, it was a political statement.

The music you listened to, raved to and protested to *defined* your identity. As Chuck D would later say of hip-hop being 'CNN for black people', calypso, soca and reggae were the BBC for Caribbean folk. For a diaspora spread across all corners of the globe, music is the art form of choice; an Esperanto that binds black peoples from Africa, the Caribbean, Europe and America together.

Maintaining a connection to the Caribbean was something Dad felt strongly about. For many people, however, going 'back a yard' was nigh on a once-in-a-lifetime event.

When I used to go back to Trinidad, because of the history of shadism in the Caribbean, the locals wouldn't see me as black. To them, on account of my fairish complexion, I was 'red man'. I'd be like, 'Red man?' I knew what a red man was back home in the UK, and I weren't no red man. Again, as a black kid growing up in the '70s and '80s, this just added to a sense of confusion about identity. One minute I was railing against people who hated me for the colour of my skin, the next I was trying to prove myself to those who I thought were my colour, my culture, but who saw me as foreign or alien. I was neither fish nor fowl.

The first time I went to Trinidad was with Dad, aged eleven. Previously, I'd been to Morocco on a youth club trip and on a school trip and a seaside holiday with Mum. But apart from this, holidays seldom featured in my childhood.

Because we left before the summer holidays had started, I wound up having to do some of my exams in Trinidad during the summer break. The first week was wicked, but the following five were like pulling teeth. All I wanted to do was go home and hang out with my mates in Fulham. Historically, we never went on holiday, so perhaps spending that much time away from my creature comforts was too much of a chore. This wasn't a holiday packed full of theme parks, adventures, waterslides and all that. Most of the time I'd be dragged off into the home of some extended family or grown-ups who seemed alien to me. Holidays just weren't a thing among West Indian families back in the day. The cost of flying four or five or six people to the Caribbean every year was way beyond the reach of most black families, so many of the Windrush generation of whom my father was part only ever took their family 'back home' once in their lifetime.

That first trip to Trinidad was an eye-opener. I was this gawky black British kid going 'back-a-yard' for the first time, which for some reason my father found a source of amusement, given the culture shock it provoked in me. He always used to tell a story, which I'm certain he made up, that on the first night we got there and I was offered something to eat, I called it 'jungle bunny food'. To this day, I don't know why he told that story or where he got it from, but it served as an apocryphal tale of how westernised or English I was. I guess in some ways it's like working-class people who rib their upwardly mobile kids for being bougie: it's a cheap shot at pretentiousness and a reminder not to forget your roots.

Dad and I stayed in my grandmother's house, the same one he grew up in with his brothers and sisters. The sitting room – or front room, as West Indians like to call it – was covered in protective plastic – the sofa, armchairs, carpets, the lot. It was like the room being put in bubble wrap in preparation for shipping off somewhere. As an added layer of protection, no one was allowed in there without express permission – certainly no one under the age of twenty-one. You just couldn't walk in the front room like you owned the joint. You weren't allowed through the front room, just like you weren't allowed to go and help yourself to what was in the fridge. Old-school West Indians had a very

Victorian attitude towards kids insofar as we were to be seen and not heard – and the less of both the better.

I shared a room upstairs with my cousin, Amoa, which was accessible via a shortcut through the front room beyond which you could access a winding staircase to the first floor. To do this I'd have to creep on my tiptoes like something out of a *Tom & Jerry* cartoon, because if Mama heard me she'd go absolutely ballistic. Those old black people weren't playing.

One day, I was having a water fight with Amoa out in the garden using one of those water tanks that would get filled once a day for supplies as there was no mains water supply. Mama must have heard us laughing and screaming from upstairs in her room. She was essentially confined to her room because of a condition that made her legs swollen, so Amoa had to attend to her daily needs, from washing her to preparing her meals. He even had to put Mama to bed at night and wake her up in the morning. I remember being woken up at some ungodly hour like 4 a.m. by Amoa.

'What are you doing?' I said, Mr Sandman burrowing my eyes.

'Doing the chores,' Amoa replied, busying himself with breakfast and the cleaning, all of which he had to do before getting himself ready for school.

Prior to that point, I didn't even know what 4 a.m. looked like. But likewise, when he got back from school, Amoa would have to do more housework before he could even entertain the idea of going out.

Anyway, there we were, whooping it up with our water fight, when I heard, 'Amoa, Darcus!!!' The pair of us trudged upstairs, sheepishly, shuffled over to Mama's bedroom and slowly pushed her door ajar.

'Come here,' she said. 'What the rasshole are you doing?'

'Having a water fight,' we replied, trying to put on the butter-wouldn't-melt-in-the-mouth routine. This wasn't going to fly.

'Cho! You're wasting the water. Amoa, get di stick.'

Without hesitation, Amoa went over to the corner of the room, where a long baton was propped up against the wall, which he gave to Mama, and she then starts giving him a good hiding. I was like, 'Dang!'

'Now, Darcus, you come here,' she barked.

'Hell, no!' I screamed before turning on my heels and taking off, out the room, along the corridor, down the stairs, and out of the house, quick time.

After finding Dad, I could see that he was going nuts. Clearly, regardless of what had warranted the original beating, he was of the mind that I didn't deserve extra licks for fleeing from my gran. He was prone to fits of anger, likely because he had been subjected to beatings himself. However, Dad was determined not to follow that path; he never laid a hand on his children because of the hidings he had gotten from his folks. Sometimes, I almost wished he had, because his long-winded, overblown lectures could be even more punishing.

He was staunchly against corporal punishment, and this led to a falling-out with Granny. She wanted to discipline me with a piece of wood, but both Dad and I were vehemently against it. This caused a major rift in the family, with me firmly stating that it wasn't how we did things where I came from. The situation remained unresolved, with both sides basically agreeing to disagree.

Walking around Trinidad with Dad taught me some practical lessons, too, about the Caribbean culture. He had a habit of breaking big bills into smaller ones so that he could give change to people he met along the way, whether they were acquaintances or strangers. Later, when I would take my own family to Trinidad and move around the streets, I'd make sure I had a wad of bills broken down into small notes for whenever I needed to give someone a bung.

As I later visited Trinidad, I remembered Dad's experiences and insights. I learned about the reality of the ghetto, the true meaning of 'killers', and how gang culture pervaded certain neighbourhoods. My family originated from East Dry River, the capital Port of Spain's first suburb, Belmont, which originally was popular with the black professional classes and today remains a middle-class area, albeit one that's seen slightly better days. Nearby areas such as Laventille had become known for their gang activities. Dad's friends often had ties to these gangs, the like of which were often associated with steel pan culture. In Dad's case, as a member of the Renegades steel pan outfit, invariably he was affiliated to the gang culture located in and around the band's pan yard and their territory.

On another trip to Trinidad, we had to visit the police station to bail out Dad's godson, whose nickname was 'Sadist'. He was the one who taught me how to handle a hatchet, which was the weapon of choice in those days. Yeah, the clue was in his name. Here I was, a spotty-faced kid, learning from a local 'badjohn' how to serve someone up, just the way he had done to his rivals. I wasn't even in my teens yet, but this side of Port of Spain made me acutely aware of the harsh realities of life on the streets in the Caribbean, and how tame the 'mean streets' of Fulham were in comparison.

I'd often hear tales about local legends and 'faces' then meet them and realise that they were actually friends or acquaintances of Dad. But here's the thing: these characters were genuinely kind, warm-hearted and sweet as pie. They weren't intimidating or threatening or came across as gangsters. They were just people who did what they had to do to survive. Aside from whatever skulduggery they were up to, they were just regular people. That's the paradox of living in a neighbourhood like ours, the ghetto: it's rough, it's tough, but it's still a community, still a place that people call 'home'.

In the old days, because so many people knew Dad, it was fine for me to walk around the ghetto or off the beaten track without any trouble. I'd be greeted warmly, and everything was cool. But today, with so much time having passed since Dad's era, I wouldn't even think of venturing into those same neighbourhoods. People get killed for stepping on the wrong crack in the pavement nowadays. The ghetto is no longer a place, it's a state of mind; and that state of mind has been corrupted by everything from drug trafficking to political shenanigans.

Nevertheless, I love Trinidad. I love the way Trinis sing. I love the way they dress. I love the way they carry themselves with a certain swagger. I love the way they get angry. I love the way they *look* like they're angry even when they're not. Trinidad is a mass of contradictions, a place where everything is a performance and nothing is ever as it seems. Much like most people, I guess.

3

You Got the Love

Sometimes I feel like throwing my hands up in the air
I know I can count on you
Sometimes I feel like saying 'Lord, I just don't care'
But you've got the love I need to see me through

– Florence + The Machine[1]

I hadn't quite reached the stage of buying full albums yet; I was still very much into collecting 7-inch records. Those small vinyl records were probably priced around 99 pence, and back then, even having a pound note was quite precious. The first thing you'd typically want to spend it on was buying some sweets to get a sugar rush. Occasionally, I'd get record tokens for my birthday or Christmas. Every time I got a card with record tokens inside, I was like Charlie ripping apart that Wonka Bar and finding the last golden ticket. I was ten years old when I got my first

---

[1] Anthony B. Stephens, Jamie Principle, Anthony Harris, John P. Bellamy Jr; Island Records.

big money record token. The very first record I bought was *The Specials* album by the Specials. It wasn't a single, nor a 7-inch; it was a whole album. My musical graduation. Despite not having a record player of my own to play it on, it was something that changed my whole life.

I was never allowed to touch the record player at home, so I would take my record round to like-minded friends' houses and play it there. I was always amazed at what white kids could do in their homes. They had sleepovers, broke shit, and never got in trouble. They could swear in front of their parents and not get boxed round the head, help themselves to food from the fridge, and most importantly, they could play records on their parents' sound systems. At our house, I'd have to sneakily wait until Mum and Dad were out or just before Mum got home from work to play records. I'd keep the volume down just in case either of them showed up unexpectedly, and make sure nothing like the little brush for the needle or the arm on the deck was out of place so I wouldn't get caught out. In some ways, as a kid, treating music in such a subversive way just added to its mystery and intrigue.

In my family home growing up, calypso music was a staple. We'd listen to the Mighty Sparrow, Byron Lee and the Drag-onaires, and Trinidadian legend David Rudder. He was one of Dad's all-time favourites. My parents had a diverse record collection that included Marvin Gaye, Big Youth, Bob Marley, and the Mighty Diamonds. At the same time, because of my parents' backgrounds, we were very much in tune with records that had political themes. So even from a very young age, from eight years old, I was singing along to complex, political lyrics by artists like Linton Kwesi Johnson just as much as I was the records in the top forty. That's why the Specials and their two-tone music came at the right time for me. While Eric Clapton had tried his best with a version of the 1973 Bob Marley classic, 'I Shot the Sheriff', the Police had stormed the charts with their 'unique' brand of reggae, and artists like the Clash, Elvis Costello, and even 10cc put out notable reggae-infused efforts, they weren't as culturally immersive or impactful as two-tone was. The likes of the Specials, the Selector, the Beat and by extension UB40, who weren't strictly two-tone but nevertheless a 'conscious' British reggae band, served as a bridge between the culturally and politically charged music we listened to at home and the mainstream chart hits, because two-tone was the perfect storm – an amazing amalgam of ska, rocksteady, reggae, punk and new wave that spoke to the nascent black British experience.

I still get an emotional response with music, regardless of the medium I hear it on. My son's generation calls records 'songs'; and old farts like me still call songs 'records'. But whether it's tape, vinyl, minidisc, CD or magically streamed out of thin air and straight into your ears, listening to music is the same; it's a timeless experience. What's different now is the way the business interacts with and monetises the emotional connection between the music and the listener, and ultimately between the artist and the fan.

In the past, you had to invest time and effort to acquire a song you'd heard on the radio. Route one was hearing it on Radio 1's weekly chart show. Here, you'd get the title, artist, everything. Sorted. But even getting a regular pop chart tune was a mission. There was no instant button-pressing, Spotify-in-seconds way of getting music. You had to get out there, onto the street, locate, travel, track that shit down. Buying records was like big game hunting. Anything obscure or not played on commercial radio was an even bigger expedition. You had to save up pocket money because the cost of records was disproportionately high, relatively to whatever spends your parents gave you – or you perhaps earned – as a teenager. You had to *invest* in records – money, time, energy, risk (some of the best record shops back in the day were in pretty sketchy parts of town) – traipse across London by bus, tube and train to trawl through racks and racks of vinyl in mega-record stores such as HMV or Tower Records or high street shops like Woolies or tucked-away, specialist record shops like Black Market Records in Soho. Sometimes you'd have to wait days or weeks to get your hands on a record which you may have heard just fleetingly on a pirate radio station and had no idea of its title or who made it. So, you'd try to sing it or hum it to friends in the hope they'd heard it, too. They'd look at you like you'd lost your marbles, roll up a spliff and carry on chatting shit. So, you'd pluck up the courage to bowl into a record shop and try to explain the record to a member of staff, who, like your friends (albeit sober), would also think that you'd lost your mind because unless you had a voice like Aretha or the doo-doo-doo skills of George Benson, however you related it with your tone-deaf ear would sound nothing like the tune you were trying to convey.

And then, just as you were about to give up and think you'd have to wait for the musical carousel to spin around in your direction at some random point in the future and give you another shot of your very own version of *Name That Tune*, a complete stranger queuing up behind you would pipe up, 'I know that tune. It's "After the Dance Is Through" by Krystol. It's on an Epic import . . .'

Finally, you'd get that coveted record home, take it carefully out of the plastic bag, then peel it out of its shrink wrap like it was the Christmas present to end all Christmas presents. And you'd play that sucker repeatedly, flipping the needle, replaying it again and again and again and again . . .

Today, the process is more instantaneous with digital access, but the emotional impact of the music remains unchanged. The industry's transformation doesn't diminish the pursuit of greatness or the deep emotional connection people have with music; it simply requires adapting to new ways of monetising and connecting with that emotion. My task, and the challenge for anyone in the music business – regardless of whether they're an artist or in A&R – is how do you consistently, and sustainably, replicate that old-school, analogue, tactile connection to music in a new-school, digital, and often transient way?

I wasn't sitting there listening to pop acts like Bay City Rollers, Mud, or Donny Osmond, or buying *Smash Hits* and *Melody Maker*. Nah, man. For me to listen to, and identify with, something that was in the charts it has to resonate with what we were listening to at home. So when the Specials' 'Ghost Town' hit the charts in 1981, I was like, wow, this joins up the dots. I desperately wanted to be part of the two-tone scene over in Ladbroke Grove but Mum wouldn't let me go there on my own, so I could only get over there when there was something happening with Carnival or Mum and Dad had a radical activist meeting to go to. While they were putting the world to rights, I would slink off to local ska nights that would be put on in old freight containers, dive bars and illegal drinking clubs. When I was really young, they wouldn't let me in, so I'd stand by the door listening to the music or try to sneak a peek through the window at what was going on inside.

At other times, I'd get dragged off to blues or 'big people's' parties by my parents, which could be anywhere across London. As it was neither in our culture nor finances to employ babysitters, as a rule, we'd get piled into a friend's car or a minicab (neither of my parents could drive), carted off to the party, where I'd get shoved upstairs, usually with a bunch of other polyester-clad kids jumping up and down frantically on an Everest of coats piled up on a bed while knocking back gallons of fizzy pop. At the beginning of the evening, it'd be all fun and games, but as the night wore on and the kids started to tire, I'd be begging my mum to go home. Of course, this is when the fun would really start for the grown-ups, and I'd know I was in for a long night. As the smell of hard liquor, perfume, aftershave, smoke and West Indian food wafted upstairs, and the thumping bass of reggae music reverberated around the house, I'd slowly drift off to this carnival of smells and sounds, with a bunch of siblings, cousins or random kids similarly passed out around me. The next thing I'd know was being woken up the following morning, piled back into the car, semi-conscious, for the long drive home. On occasion, we'd get stopped by the police of course, pulled out of the car, and left to shiver on the pavement while they filled out the inevitable 'producer' – a routine form of police harassment that inspired reggae artist and DJ Smiley Culture's hit, 'Police Officer'.[2]

Blues parties and shebeens were an essential part of the black British experience, pretty much since the dawn of the Windrush

---

[2] In the UK, an HORT/1 form, commonly known as a 'producer', is issued to motor vehicle drivers who are unable to produce their driving licence and insurance and MOT certificates when stopped by a police officer. The driver then has seven days to produce said documents at a police station of their choice for verification.

generation in 1948. A colour bar meant that black people were prohibited from going to most dancehalls, nightclubs, and even later, discos, apart from in dribs and drabs or accompanied by white guests with some pull. Still today, informal colour bars exist to stop sizeable groups of black people from attending venues, or hiring them for private parties, even in places that routinely place black music. Growing up, I never saw my parents go nightclubbing. Blues parties were their thing.

When I came of age, house parties were still happening, but now I was old enough to go clubbing. My best friend, KG, who was a DJ and in a rap group, wound up getting a record deal. It was hanging out with him at his DJing gigs that piqued my interest in the music business. I was just curious about how it all worked. I was like, 'Oh shit. So, there's a record label that you're signed to that puts out your records? And this is what happens? And that's the process?' But I didn't have an ambition to be in the music industry as such – and certainly not to be famous. I was just hungry to know more about the mechanics of it now that the lid on the business was being opened. But it was also about finding a deeper connection. Music was much more than just entertainment for me. It had profound significance in my life, offering structure, solace and comfort amid all the chaos.

For me, two-tone was a way to relate to a fusion of mainstream and black music that wasn't just about catchy tunes like Boney M. or 'Feeling Hot Hot Hot' but substance, depth and soul, if you will.

People often mistakenly associate black music with black record buyers having a narrow band of musical tastes and influences. This couldn't be further from the truth. It wasn't unusual back then, and still now, for many West Indians to have a mix of country and western, classical, opera, rock 'n' roll, old crooners and show tune records alongside their John Holt, Dennis Brown, Beres Hammond, and Lord Kitchener 12-inches, backed up by a substantive amount of black American music. A lot of West Indian artists would take those country songs and give them a reggae twist. Dad being Dad, of course, never dug country music. He was deep into his Darcus Owusu Black Power phase at that point, so I never saw any Tammy Wynette or Dolly Parton records in our collection. My parents were all about the green combat, Bob Marley rebel vibe at that time, with a dose of lovers' rock thrown in.

My palate for music, however, was broadening. Going round to white friends' houses to use their record players to play my shit meant that not only did I get to hear what they had to offer, I could rummage through their parents' record collections, too. From a young age, I was listening to Led Zeppelin and Wishbone Ash. I understood what punk was. A couple of times, in the middle of the night, Dad showed up at the flat with John Lydon, the pair having been on the lash. I'd think, *Shit, that's Johnny Rotten!* I knew about John Cooper Clarke from an early age and Ian Dury and the Blockheads were on my radar too, Linton having toured with Ian. My concept of musical hybridity was formed very early on because I was immersed in a world where black and white music that raged against the machine coalesced. Most of my friends, however, didn't get this about me. Often they'd say, with slack-jawed ignorance, 'What the fuck are you listening to?' I didn't care, though. As far as I was concerned there were only two types of music in the world: good music and shit music. If it was good music, the genre was immaterial.

So, there I am, growing up with the soundtrack to my parents' generational experience in one ear and the developing sound of second-generation Black Britain in the other, both of which were set against a backdrop of social unrest, upheaval and eclectic musical influences coming from different directions and sources. Patently, I wasn't naïve to race; I wasn't naïve to racism; and I wasn't naïve to the political interplay between the two and a mainstream British public, which could be duped into turning on a sixpence against people like me thanks to the rhetoric being shoved down their throats by the Thatcher regime. I didn't realise it at the time but slowly but surely, I was inching my way towards understanding that one of the most powerful ways to counteract political and racist propaganda is through music.

I didn't have to know that Willie Whitelaw was the home secretary or who the rest of Thatcher's cabinet were to be aware of how nasty British politics was back then. My house was full of enough discourse, debate and, yes, protest music to know what the state of the nation was. And when I wasn't getting it in the ear at Mum's place, which Dad had slowly drifted away from, I'd get it from being in his friends' company or at his uncle C.L.R.'s house in Brixton. Occasionally, he'd take me round to the great scribe – who among many works had authored the critically acclaimed definitive history of the Haitian revolution, *The Black Jacobins* – and while the pair put the world to rights in animated fashion, I'd sit silently in a corner of his study, which was more like an antiquarian bookshop or the national archive of a small republic than a typical urban sitting room.

As a kid, I saw Mum's struggles and Dad's determination to make a better life, and I felt compelled to make something meaningful out of my own life, but formal education was something that never really clicked for me.

'Darcus, why is your favourite word "sorry"?' Mum would often say, sarcastically, pointing to the fact that I was constantly in trouble at school, on the street, and at home and thus constantly saying 'sorry' for one screw-up or another. I wasn't so bad that I was ever suspended or expelled, but I was frequently thrown out of the class for low-level disruption. Also, I was inclined to drop the shoulder without warning. People would turn around and go, 'Where's Darcus?' I would just disappear. I would just go. I was that guy. Turn around and I'm not there. I'd be super annoying. I just operated completely differently to most of my friends and peers; I was wired differently. Very differently.

An example of how this undetected but clearly odd 'wiring' would manifest itself, even when I was a small boy, occurred one day when I was still at primary school. I had been in the playground at lunchtime playing marbles with another kid and we'd got into an argument over some silliness. Seeing the kerfuffle, the school keeper came over and decided to confiscate the marbles. Nothing wrong there, you might think. Certainly, this minor spat would've long faded from memory were it not for the fact that my mum dug up a letter some years ago about the incident, which the school keeper had written to the headmaster, a copy of which was sent to my parents. 'While I was in the playground there was a bit of trouble with Darcus and some children over marbles,' the school keeper writes. 'I said to them, give me the marbles and you can pick them up from Mr Gray [the headmaster]. Then Darcus turned around and said, "No, you cunt!"' It wasn't that I was a horrible kid – on the contrary, in fact. But I was seen as disruptive, a pattern that began from a young age, and like many young black boys, it was a reputation that I found difficult to shake. For a long time, I assumed my railing against authority was a result of witnessing my parents battling against the powers that be. And yes, some of that may have been a contributory factor. However, I have since learned that my behaviours were typical of a boy with ADHD. So, I was undiagnosed and misunderstood. How many others have suffered the same fate?

Then there was this one time when, at about eleven or twelve years old, I got my hands on what people used to call 'blues' – speed tablets. Me and some pals were doing 'penny for the Guy', roaming around Fulham, speeding off our faces. One of Mum's friends saw me on Fulham Broadway around 10 p.m. that night and shouted at me to get home. As I rounded the corner to my house, a police car pulled up outside my yard with its 'blues and twos' on. Next stop, A&E, where I was forced to drink half my body weight in water. Mum was 'vex'! It often feels like my success was far from predestined, like, this shit just wasn't meant to happen. Apart from my parents' love and DNA, there was nothing to suggest that I'd ever be a success. Mum and Dad had a right to worry about how I was going to turn out.

Mum used to go next door to use the neighbour's phone as we didn't have one in our house. She'd put 10p in a pot by the phone, which was on a stand just inside their front door. Whenever I got in trouble at school or on the street she would roar, 'I'm going to call your dad.' He wasn't living with us by then, but he'd often show up at random times or, if Mum phoned him, he'd heed the call, stop what he was doing and make a beeline for me. He wasn't what you'd call a hands-on father – the only thing he seemed to care about was my education, my running and my behaviour. But the moment all hell broke loose he'd turn up, incandescent with rage.

I think with Dad, in the first instance, my emotional response to him was fear, followed by intimidation, then respect. Love came later. Much later. With Mum, it was always about love and respect. Eventually, I got to a point where I could say, 'Oh, shut up, Dad,' because I no longer sought his attention or approval. That was liberating.

One day, a teacher said to me, 'Darcus, you know what? Your energy is misplaced. Why don't you run around the playground and see how many times you can do it?' And that's how running became my go-to form of meditation. At school I was told time and time again that I was 'never going to make it'. All my reports confirmed as much, too. But luckily, while running would become a calming influence on my hyperactive self, music was something that I could hyper-focus on. It would take a long time to understand what was going on in my head, but patently I was, to use the modern parlance, 'on the spectrum'. This seemed to be the case for many kids, especially black kids – a significant minority of whom were disabled by the way they saw, felt and experienced life. But for a minority within the minority, such 'disabilities' were not a problem. Far from it. If you could harness that energy, redirect it, use it, it was in fact a superpower.

It was around this time that I first started to get cluster headaches, an excruciating, rare form of headache that comes in recurring, throbbing bouts that can last up to three hours and come and go for a good three months. Known as 'suicide headaches' due to the dark thoughts the intense pain can bring about, one night, I woke up in the wee hours with my head banging, the pain increasing with ceaseless intensity. By the morning, with no sign of the headache relenting, Mum was beside herself, thinking I may have a brain tumour, so she took me off to nearby Charing

Cross Hospital where doctors in the neurology department mis-diagnosed me as suffering from cluster migraines. I wouldn't say that their advice was as crude as 'take two aspirin and get some rest' but it wasn't far off.

Every year, these 'alarm-clock headaches' would come with such frequency that I'd be afraid to go to sleep. I knew that when I was 'in season' I'd be awoken in the middle of the night by an intense pounding in my hypothalamus, the part of the brain that's the main link between your endocrine system and your nervous system. Put in plain English, the hypothalamus is what keeps your shit together, so the only way to numb the pain and stop myself from going mad – or wanting to jump under a train – was to pop every painkiller that I could buy over the counter.

Mum's concerns were about the future of her black son. She knew what they were fighting for back then, and she wanted the next generation, like me, to have a fair chance and a level playing field. It's incredible to think about her worries and the fact that nothing was laid out for young black men at the time. We weren't encouraged to pursue tech courses or go to university. At school careers and further education meetings the most we were ever offered was a BTech in catering. I knew I wanted something out of life, but at the time I didn't have a clear sense of what that 'something' would be. Looking back, I can see that there was an undeniable drive within me, a sense that I couldn't settle for mediocrity, even if I wasn't sure what success looked like. I always had this belief that I would succeed in some way or another. The challenge was that my path to success wasn't going to be through a traditional school–sixth form–university education. With parents like mine, it was highly unlikely that I'd become Employee of the Month at McDonald's any time soon, so something had to give.

Despite having half-brothers and half-sisters, who I've always been close to, I was Mum's only child and thus was raised as an only child. My siblings from my father were all parented in pairs. Tamara, Taipha, Rap, Clare, Amiri and Zoe all had each other, and all my friends growing up came from large families with loads of brothers and sisters in the same house. But circumstances made me a loner. Because Mum was working all the hours under the sun, and when she wasn't working she was out campaigning, I was often left at home to my own devices. While some kids in the same situation would take comfort in reading, playing the guitar, watching TV, doing keepy-uppies in the garden, or some other solitary activity, I would spend hour after hour listening to music, and I did so in a completely different way to how I knew my friends or family listened to pop music, mainly because I noticed that they seemed more engaged with the music, whereas what really interested me were the lyrics. Music spoke to me. Lyrics spoke to me. It was almost like a companion, a companion that I took around with me in my Sony Walkman, and a little handheld stereo. Music was like a friend to me.

It's fair to say that my path wasn't as clearly charted as those of many white middle-class or even working-class families in the UK. When I was growing up, white people's lives seemed predetermined compared with the chaos in my world. They had a much clearer idea of where they were going to work or be further educated, what they'd inherit and how their futures would unfold. Their parents, and their parents' parents typically, set up a well-defined roadmap for them. But, likewise, Mum and Dad's experiences, black people's experiences, period, not only shaped their perspective, they influenced the way they prepared us, their sons and daughters, for life. They aimed to equip us with the tools to *survive* as opposed to thrive. I realise that a significant part of my baggage comes from my parents: willingness to take a stand on certain issues, whether right or wrong. This trait was instilled in me from an early age.

So, I was listening to John Lydon and Public Image, to 'Too Much Too Young' by the Specials, to Linton Kwesi Johnson's 'Inglan Is a Bitch' before I was a teenager. I wasn't listening to 'Hey fatty boom-boom. Sweet sugar dumpling' and all that. My introduction to music was serious. When people say they were brought up on Nat King Cole and Frank Sinatra, or Billie Holiday or blah, blah, blah, that wasn't me. I was all about the Specials. They were the first band that reflected what me and my mates looked like. I looked down my street and we were black, white and brown and that was the first time you looked at a band and it was a mixed, multicultural band. Once I'd scrimped and saved enough money, I bought into all the two-tone, rude boy paraphrenia: the tonic suit, the pork pie hat, the Crombie, the loafers. *The Specials* by the Specials was like my Bible.

I guess the theatricality of two-tone, and youth culture in general at the time, combined with my boundless energy pushed me ever more in a creative direction. Seventies and '80s London was like one big set from *The Warriors*. You had gangs of punks, skinheads, rude boys, casuals, new romantics, Rastas, clones, soul boys, B-boys, goths, Sloanes, yuppies, buppies, mods, rockers, psycho-billies . . . everyone seemed to dress like they came straight out of Central Casting, so for a while I aspired to be a dancer or an actor after dabbling with American tap and auditioned for several stage schools and musicals, including Italia Conti and *Bugsy Malone*. The only problem was, I was no Sammy Davis Jr. I just didn't have enough talent to get into a stage or performing arts school.

Oddly enough, one evening while at my sister Taipha's house, we got talked into doing a 'turn' by the oldies, that form of parlour or indoor entertainment that was common among West Indian and Irish folk. Everyone, especially the kids, had to have a party trick or joke or performative talent they could put on show at the click of a finger, or else you'd be dead meat. A common turn was to do a skit, which basically you could improv on the spot if you didn't have an actual talent that involved playing an instrument. I had tried my hand at the saxophone, but given my levels of concentration and interest in lyrics more than musicianship, I was never going to master anything beyond the triangle.

Anyway, for some reason, I grabbed someone's trilby, put on a pair of glasses, a loud purple satin shirt with the collar turned up and pretended to be a music manager who discovers Taipha and her friend busking on the street. It was literally a joke, and everyone laughed their socks off at the ridiculousness of it, which I got off on. Despite being a loner and enjoying my own company, I also liked being the centre of attention – something, again, which came from being the mascot on so many demos at such a young age. But the thought of being a big cheese in the music industry, let alone running one of the most iconic record labels in the history of iconic record labels, had never entered my head. Let's not be stupid here: things like that didn't happen to people like me.

Perhaps Dad's 'performances' had also rubbed off on me, albeit in a more abstract, creative way. While I was still at school, his broadcasting career began on the Afrocentric Channel 4 current affairs series, *Black on Black*, then moved on to co-editing the more multicultural current affairs series *The Bandung File*, before presenting another hard-hitting series, again for Channel 4, which would make him a household name, followed by the *Daily Mail*'s worst nightmare, *Devil's Advocate*. As the name suggests, Dad would 'challenge conventional wisdom about a major talking point of the day' by subjecting a guest or group of people occupying the 'Hot Seat' to a thorough grilling and added interrogation by a generally spiky audience. In one now-legendary episode, Dad caught the former MP for Tottenham, and something of a friend, Bernie Grant, in a lie over comments he had made during a Labour Party Conference fringe meeting in 1993, in which Grant had supported state-funded 'voluntary repatriation'. Armed with a tape of the meeting, Dad exposed Grant. Cue: much backsliding.

Dad argued, '. . . just when we thought we had established our rights here as British citizens, Bernie has offered us the defeatist position of abandoning ship with our pockets filled with silver.' As the book *Darcus Howe: A Political Biography* noted, 'voluntary repatriation was the beginning of a slippery slope that would inevitably lead to forced repatriation. Howe offered an alternative slogan, borrowed from an Asian anti-racist demonstration of the time, 'They say "Get Back" we say, "Fight Back!"'. Dad wanted black people in Britain to be afforded all the rights, benefits and freedoms of their white countryfolk. Repatriation to the Caribbean or Africa, at any cost, was out of the question.

One of the rights I'd been afforded growing up was of course free education. When I left Henry Compton School for Boys, which is also the alma mater of the former British sprinter Linford Christie and World Cup-winning footballer George Cohen, I knew I wanted to do something creative because patently I was a frustrated or closet performer. However, I had no qualifications to speak of. Having flunked most of my exams that June, I had a summer ahead of me with zero prospect of further education or a job. As I had gotten into middle-distance running, I thought I could go to Loughborough College, study sports science and become a PE teacher, but the reality was I was never academically smart enough to go on to university. 'Don't put yourself down,' Mum would say, trying to encourage me to get back into studying. But I just lacked the application. Mum was academic, Dad was academic, and my eldest sister Tamara was academic. I just didn't have it.

'Well, Darcus, you're not going to sit around here and do nothing,' Mum said. 'Go and get a bloody job!'

As an activist, she knew how hard it was for young black men to find employment, so naturally she was worried about how I was going to fare, even if I didn't seem to give a shit. Pulling out all the stops, one day she suggested I go see her former hair-dresser, who had a posh salon on Kensington Church Street. Mum had known the dude since the Swinging Sixties, which was when he first started cutting her massive Angela Davis super 'fro.

'Go and see him, have an interview, and get some experience job hunting,' Mum said.

I fixed myself up, went to the salon, had an interview, and as luck would have it, I got a job sweeping up hair. It was great. It was the Lady Diana era, so all these rich white women with their big Lady Diana hair would come into the salon, some of them every day, because they were filthy rich and didn't have jobs.

Whenever the reception phone rang and I went to answer it, I'd get brushed out of the way.

'Why won't you let me answer the phone?' I'd ask, naïvely.

'Because you can't speak properly' would come the response. I was baffled.

'Darcus, sweetheart, when you pick up the phone at a business you have to speak properly, and use *all* of the vowels . . .'

I'd never had to 'speak proper' in all my life. So, after that, the mission then wasn't to learn how to cut hair, it was, 'How the hell am I going to answer this phone?!' All I wanted was to be able to answer the phone and meet clients at the door, neither of which I ever got the chance to do, because all I could do at the time was just wash hair and sweep up. Now I was on a mission: I wanted to get noticed.

I worked in the Kensington salon for a year, but I got it in my head that it wasn't trendy enough for me, so I ended up moving to another salon, in Monmouth Street, Seven Dials, right in the centre of Covent Garden, in 'London's fashionable West End' as game-shows back in the day used to call it. This new salon was a much sassier place run by three hairdressers, one of whom, Rebecca, had trained under the hairdresser to the stars, Daniel Galvin, and in turn took me under her wing and taught me how to colour. Jeff Banks of BBC One's *The Clothes Show* fame wound up backing her to start her own salon, so taking me with her as her assistant, we set up shop, initially in her home. If it wasn't for Rebecca, I would never have got into the music industry. She was my maven.

Colouring, colouring, and more frigging colouring. Stepping into this new environment was both exhilarating and daunting.

Being up town I found myself in a hotbed of fashion, creativity, artistry and yes, music. Through Rebecca, I started connecting with people who were into music and fashion – but not as punters or spectators. They worked on the industry side of those worlds. Now, through exposure to those worlds, I was developing an eye as well as an ear for what clicked, what worked, and what flopped. The people I'd meet in the salon were an early version of what we now call 'influencers', which back in the day marketers used to call 'trendsetters' and then 'early adopters'. These were the cats who just had a knack for knowing what was cool, what was happening, and what could blow up from being a niche, underground fad into a mainstream commercial success. This is when I first realised that having an ear and eye, what you might call 'taste' or curatorial nous, was a skill in itself. Being able to gauge and forecast what was going to make waves in the world over the next six months, year, or three years. These early adopters that came into the salon somehow knew how to shape opinions and trends. Networking, showing off and influencing were what it's all about. I started to think that maybe I should embrace some of this myself and be more confident, rather than indulge myself in being just another 'Who, me?' wannabe who'd soon be chewed up, spat out and kicked to the kerb of life.

It was time for action.

4

Started From the Bottom

I done kept it real from the jump
Living at my mama house we'd argue every month
Nigga, I was tryna get it on my own
Workin' all night, traffic on the way home

— Drake[1]

The ground-zero moment that shaped my career in the music industry was an unexpected stroke of luck that led to a life-changing opportunity. As a young record collector, I used to spend endless hours trawling through record shops all over London buying vinyl, blagging vinyl, and was always eager to get my hands on the latest releases. My expanding network and friendships had blossomed out of Rebecca's salon, where I had eventually become a fully fledged colourist working on models for Jeff Banks' *The Clothes Show* on BBC One, and as a result I found

---

[1] Aubrey Graham, Noah Shebib and Michael Coleman; Young Money Entertainment.

myself connected to more and more people in the fashion and music industries, including two fellas who used to get their hair cut at Rebecca's who happened to work for Island Records.

I started getting invites to showbiz and music industry parties. It was all fairground rides, burnt-out cars, vodka fountains – mad '80s shit, spiky hairdos, big shoulder pads, flash, pizazz. After hanging out with these Island boys for a while, at the end of one evening out on the lash, one of them mentioned, casually, that they were going to a party being thrown by Elton John's manager, John Reid. I was like, *Elton John's manager?* Here I was, just an eighteen-year-old kid rocking up at this fancy party; it was a surreal moment. But the idea of rubbing shoulders with famous people felt incredibly intoxicating. I wanted some of this. I'd obviously made some sort of impression as, the following week, one of the Island boys, Julian, invited me to their HQ at 22 St Peter's Square, Chiswick, which was located in a big Victorian townhouse. As I walked round to his office, hoping at the very least to blag some records, I ran into his friend and colleague, Bernie.

'Hey, all right, Darcus? What are you doing here? Are you looking for a job?'

'What, me?' I replied cautiously.

'A kid in the promotions department has literally just handed in his notice. You should go and see the other Julian. He's head of promotions. Maybe he can hook you up?'

The following day, I bunked off from the salon and hurried back to Island's office, saw Julian from promotions and mentioned Bernie's name, hoping for a chance to work at the label. It was a bit of a long shot, as getting your foot in the door of a major record label is no mean feat. Seven days later, however,

I had a job. At Island Records. Before this 'touch' I had sent out numerous CVs to various record companies but never got a response. This chance encounter had changed everything.

It was the summer of '88, the so-called 'Second Summer of Love', when I got my big break. It was an amazing time not just to be into music, but to enter the music industry. It was also the dawn of yet another golden era of black music. Genres and subgenres were popping off everywhere. The acid house and rave scene was going properly mental and redefining UK clubland while British soul was crushing it with the likes of Soul II Soul, Sade, the Brand New Heavies, Omar, Simply Red, Loose Ends and Lisa Stansfield to name a few, producing some absolute bangers. The DNA of Caribbean music, particularly reggae, dancehall, DJing and MCing, was evident in the rise and rise of rap and hip-hop culture. The likes of Grandmaster Flash, Afrika Bambaataa, DJ Kool Herc, Fab 5 Freddy, Doug E. Fresh, Busta Rhymes, Heavy D, KRS-One and a host of other artists were whole or part second-generation West Indian stock from America, which in some ways mirrored the evolution of second-generation, hybrid UK music forms, such as two-tone, jungle, and drum and bass. An array of house music from Detroit and Chicago to London and Manchester further illustrated the nexus between the UK, US and the Caribbean, the backbone of which was black music.

Protest music, too, had leapt from the niche record collections of my activist parents' generation and into the charts, with N.W.A.'s incendiary gangsta rap classic, 'Fuck Tha Police' and Public Enemy's musically and politically boundary-pushing 'Fight The Power' becoming the anthems of disaffected, rebellious youth from both sides of the Atlantic. Hip-hop was the new punk rock. Whether it was on the dancefloors or the streets, music was bringing people of all races and backgrounds together like never before.

Fortunately, timing was on my side during that period. It was probably the last year of its kind insofar as the perfect storm of social, cultural, political and musical elements had collided. Given the calibre of people I'd crossed paths with in the music industry by then, when I walked into the Island interview, I dropped a few names and gave off the instant impression that I had a solid network in the business. Once again, I was flying by the seat of my 501s, but times were a-changing, and Island was just the sort of label to embrace that.

I started out on a three-month trial in the promotions department, but shortly into it, like an idiot, some bloke wound me up and I lost my temper, nearly blowing the chance of a lifetime. I can't even remember what the row was about, but I just lost it, picked up a chair in frustration and, like a petulant teenager, was ready to throw it across the room. But in that instant, I caught myself, realising the gravity of my actions, not least because of the look of shock on the faces of everyone else in the room. I put the chair back down, thankfully saving the moment from disaster. 'You could take the boy out of Sands End but you couldn't take the Sands End out of the boy' was something I'd have to work on, and quickly.

While I was able to manage that anger and tempestuousness, others around me weren't. To a certain extent, I was able to keep a lid on the chaos because my upbringing had been a bit of a mess. I grew up in a completely different environment to those around me now. I still had a lot to learn, and part of the learning curve was knowing how to keep my shit together. I'm not making excuses for myself, or trying to sound 'chippy', but on the whole the relationship between blacks and whites has traditionally been just a touch one-sided. Sometimes, given the rage against the machine that had been instilled in me since birth, I'd lose it. As Flavor Flav rapped on Public Enemy's 'Prophets of Rage', 'I got a right to be hostile, man, my people bein' persecuted.' Thankfully, not so hostile that I lost my job before it even got started.

So, I successfully completed the trial period and secured my position at Island Records, while learning a valuable lesson: when opportunity knocks you need to be ready to run with it. What use is 'luck' if you don't capitalise on it?

This moment serves as a poignant reminder that life's course can change unexpectedly. It is a testament to the power of connections and the significance of seizing opportunities when they present themselves. My journey into the music industry started with a twist of fate, a touch of luck, but it also highlighted the importance of staying grounded and true to oneself.

But moving into the music industry was yet another leap into the unknown. Unlike traditional professions or careers, the music industry didn't fit into a neat box. It was a space where creativity, talent and innovation flourished, challenging conventional norms. It wasn't just about acquiring a set of skills, it was about embracing my unique passion and vision.

One morning, I was standing in a big open-plan office that we used to call the 'war room'. It had this massive whiteboard and one of those library-style ladders you used to shuffle up and across it. It was that big. And, of course, it was called the war room because it was the hub of operations. The managing director's office overlooked the whole room. You could see the press department, promotions and everyone else. So, this particular morning I was trying to climb up that ladder to write down the daily radio plays when Chris Blackwell walked in. He had a red, gold and green scarf draped around his neck and an energy that seemingly changed the air particles in the room. Everyone started whispering, 'Chris is on the floor, Chris is on the floor . . .' and put their heads down, pretending to work.

Chris was hardly ever in the UK at that time because he was busy building his Miami hotels and had his own island in the Bahamas, among other things. He was not long off from selling his stake in the company (he stepped down from the board in 1997), but whenever he was around, it was a big deal.

Chris was a charismatic but also intimidating figure. However, I needed to make a move and introduce myself as he only rarely appeared on the shop floor these days and word was he was selling the company.

'Hi, Chris, I'm Darcus,' I said gingerly.

'Darcus. Nice to meet you. And what do you do?'

'I'm the tea boy.'

'Really? In what department?'

I pointed towards the promotions department. He looked over at the glass-fronted office, then at me, checking me out more intently now.

'The promotions department, eh? That used to be Stiff Records.'

He then walked off. And that was the first of many magical musical history lessons I would get from Chris. It's amazing to think that that gangly tea boy with swagger back then would rise through the ranks to run one of the most iconic record labels in the world. I had no ambition – or interest – in running a record label. But, then, what eighteen-year-old does?

Back then, everyone at Island seemed to play some sort of instrument or was in a band. It also seemed as if they'd all been to university and had either studied anthropology or sociology. So, everyone around me appeared smarter and more musically inclined. I had nothing but my wits, relying solely on how I saw the world. In other words, I was blagging it.

Suddenly, here I was, working with middle-class white people in a white middle-class world that I'd never come across in my life before. From the listeners', record buyers' or gig goers' perspective, the music business seems pretty *out there*, but behind the scenes, on a corporate level, it was pretty conservative. Even at a legendary independent label such as Island, I'm not sure they'd ever come across someone like me. Certainly not in the workplace.

At the time, I felt like there was no one who reflected me or my take on the world or had walked the path I had until I started bumping into a more diverse group of people in the industry. People like Lincoln Elias, CBS/Sony Records A&R, who had become one of Rebecca's friends. Lincoln's office was round the corner from the salon and occasionally I'd pop in and blag some free records. Here was a brotha who looked like me, who was doing incredible stuff inside a major record company with Des'ree, Jamiroquai and Terence Trent D'Arby. As former Island exec Muff Winwood had said, 'Lincoln has an excellent eye and ears for talented artists. He has an inbuilt understanding of what they need to succeed – and how to go about achieving it.' I thought, *I want to be like this brotha.*

For nine or ten months, I was a lowly assistant in the promotions department. I did mail-outs, made people tea, collected their dry cleaning and was generally a gopher. Paying my dues in the early days enabled me to make the best tea, which I can do even to this day. For me, that says I paid my dues. The writer Tom Wolfe once said that the key to being a good reporter was to 'perfect the art of hanging out'. Well, in the music industry the key to success is to 'perfect the art of making a good cuppa'.

As easy as it was to give white people the side eye, the screw face, or flip 'em the bird given the world I was born into, I had to learn to knuckle down. The mainstream – i.e. white – population had the privilege of pretending that we lived in a 'tolerant' post-racial society, but that was only because they saw the world through rose-tinted spectacles. Take the shades off, open your eyes, and you'd see the world as I saw it growing up. Namely, a pretty screwed-up place. This might sound chippy but, coming from where I came from, I had to learn to understand that when a white senior member of staff at work (which was everybody) said, 'Hey, Darcus, can you get the teas in?', the answer wasn't, 'What, am I your slave?', but, 'No problem. Milk and two sugars?'

Even though I was the tea boy, I would make sure that whenever an Island band was playing, I went to see them. I would also go along with the A&R guys to see up-and-coming bands. People soon started asking my opinion about what I was seeing and hearing.

Eventually, word got around to the managing director at the time, Clive Banks, that I'd been hanging out with the A&R folks, going to gigs with them and checking out all our acts on the roster, as well as unsigned talent.

'I think you're wasted in promotions,' he said, pulling me aside. It was autumn 1988. 'You shouldn't be in that "yes man" role. I think you'd work well in the A&R department.'

It was a life-changing moment for me. I was promoted to the role of A&R scout, which was a significant shift, as usually the route up the ladder was to start off as an office assistant, then move up to become a marketing assistant or A&R assistant before becoming a scout. For those of us learning the ropes in those areas, the age range was generally nineteen to twenty-four, so I was conscious that I'd leapfrogged my peers at the label both in terms of position and age. And I hadn't even been at the label a year. I didn't start ego-tripping, but it did feel that I was making my mark. Like someone knew I existed.

In a nutshell, A&R – 'artists and repertoire' – is the division of a record label that's responsible for scouting new talent and overseeing the creative development of artists and song-writers. I always thought that these cats were the rock stars of the labels. They all drove flash whips, had expense accounts and sometimes they'd jet off to far-flung destinations, hang out with pop royalty and make records in the studio. I loved the sound of that. But I didn't think I had the chops to be an A&R person. Until now.

Let's be real: if it wasn't for Island Records and the era that I had gone in on the ground floor, things might have turned out very differently. Many of the folks I encountered while they were breaking into the music scene were university-educated, over-whelmingly white and middle class. But here I was, this black kid from a tough, white working-class neighbourhood of west London once again being outnumbered and outgunned and outlying from the rest of the crowd.

Aside from Lincoln Elias and one or two others, it was an almost exclusively white club. I have to thank Clive Banks for seeing the potential in me because I didn't see it in myself. I didn't join Island to become an A&R person. My strategy (if you could call it that) up until that point had been one of 'suck it and see'.

But here's the thing about Island Records – even though there were only a handful of black folks there, it was still a bit more diverse than most other labels. Perhaps this is no surprise given that Chris, despite being born in London in 1937, had grown up in Jamaica, the heir to the Crosse & Blackwell food empire. With family money behind him, he had been able to indulge his passion for reggae music, which he wanted to bring to the masses, and eventually did in the shape of the legendary Bob Marley. Having created Island in 1958 aged just twenty-two, Chris knew something about outliers. As a child, he suffered from chronic asthma and thus had very little contact with other kids. Just like me, he knew what it meant to feel isolated, albeit on a different level. 'I spent most of my time around nurses, gardeners or the staff in the house,' he once said, which made for a curious parallel with my own upbringing, as I had spent much of my time growing up around activists, campaigners or protestors on the street.

It took a while to appreciate it, but Chris and his assistant, Suzette Newman, who had worked with him for decades, had seemingly had their eye on me from the get-go. Once I got to know Chris, he became a great friend, mentor and even a father figure. Here was a man who had once had six records in the UK top ten. Through Island, he wrote the playbook on what a record label should look, feel and sound like. Some people had gotten into the music business to be Pete Waterman or Simon Cowell, but from the moment I met Chris Blackwell, I wanted to be Chris Blackwell.

I soon learned that I had to be strategic when it came to finding the right cultural fit. The lack of diversity in many industries, even those where you might expect more cultural representation at senior management level such as the music industry, is shocking, which is why so many businesses and sectors struggle. They don't move with the times. Even in football, which is often seen as a more diverse arena, you'll find that while 43 per cent of Premier League players and 34 per cent of Football League players in England are black, the percentage of black managers is significantly lower. At the time of writing, according to the *Washington Post*, across all four professional divisions in England 'only 4.4 per cent of managing/coaching jobs and 1.6 per cent of executive positions in the game go to black candidates'.

When I reflect on it, I can't help but feel that Island Records was always going to be closer to my heart than some other multinational labels. Ironic, then, that Universal – the Dutch–American recording behemoth – would absorb Island along with a slew of other iconic labels. And in this predominantly homogeneous, corporate landscape, I couldn't help but be preoccupied with being 'the other'. That's not to say that being an outlier was necessarily a bad thing. Once I learned how to work it to my advantage, there's always a fascinating dynamic at play when you're in a distinct minority. If you're black and you manage to break through, you essentially become the secret sauce. The mere fact that you've made it suggests there's something unique and remarkable about you because you've overcome significant barriers. People start asking, 'Who is this guy?' That's where you get the power.

But there's another facet to this. It does often rely on patronage, on a white cultural gatekeeper who's willing to take a chance on you. It's that gatekeeper who can see the potential for you to bridge the cultural gap and bring valuable expertise to the table. Sometimes it's driven by a recognition that markets are changing and you need someone who's plugged into the real deal, who knows the scene inside and out, who's an early adopter, a trendsetter, an influencer and curator. Sometimes it's about optics, PR or ticking a diversity box. I like to think that I was there on merit because I had the right arsenal of skills and attributes to be a soldier in Island's army of A&Rs. But whatever the motivation for the higher-ups seeing my potential, like any black person who gets ahead in an overwhelmingly white profession or industry, there are always going to be haters who want to rain on your parade and suggest that tokenism has played a part in your success because they're bitter, twisted and, well, racist. To those people I say: sayonara, suckers.

I might not have been old enough or aware enough at the time to question why someone like Clive Banks or Chris Blackwell was taking an interest in me. But what I can say is that if it had been another record label, things might have played out differently. But it was Island, and when I received what I considered a seal of approval, I felt like I belonged.

Within weeks of being promoted I was out at Chris's amazing Grade II-listed farmhouse and recording studio called Woolwich Green Farm, which was on 35 acres in the picturesque village of Theale in Berkshire. A&Rs from the London office, the US and other parts of the world would often assemble there for meetings. At the end of an intense day, Chris instructed his PA to inform us that he was heading off to Paris. He specifically wanted a few of us to accompany him on this trip – and I was one of the chosen ones. I remember looking around, surprised, thinking, *Wait, me?*, while clocking some equally surprised but poorly concealed expressions on the faces of a few colleagues who patently also were wondering, *Wait, Darcus?*

So, on 14 July 1989, Bastille Day, around seven or eight of us flew to Paris with Chris on a private jet for a music festival commemorating the 200th anniversary of the French Revolution, where we caught a performance by Baaba Maal, the Senegalese singer-guitarist, and of course an Island signing. It was an incredible trip. There were fireworks, celebrations – the whole nine yards. Chris flew us into Paris just for the evening to catch this music festival and then flew us back home again. Here I am, this teenage kid, still living at home with his mum, and I'm flying on a private jet. Four months later, the head of promotions asked me to fly to Hong Kong with Ladbroke Grove reggae band Aswad, who, somewhat bizarrely, were booked to perform as the headline entertainment at the Miss World show. I couldn't believe it. Between Mum, Dad and myself, we must've had every Aswad pressing from their debut album in 1976 to date. It was a major TV appearance, yet I had no prior training or experience. I was thrown in at the deep end, but I wasn't the type to be nervous or hesitant, so I just did it. It wasn't uncommon for young A&Rs to do this kind of chaperoning, which basically entailed looking after the band and making sure that, to paraphrase the famous adage, whatever happened in Hong Kong, stayed in Hong Kong.

Without a doubt, I was living my best life.

Scouting was exactly what it sounded like: you'd get out there, in the field, on the road, scouting for talent. Whether in your own whip or a company car, armed with an *A to Z* map, the mission was twofold: see as many acts as possible and, of course, rack up the miles in your company car. The catch was, you couldn't upgrade your car until you'd done 1,000 miles, so we were always on the move, planning our journeys using physical maps before the days of GPS and Google Maps.

We'd leave London with a backpack full of demo tapes and set out to different parts of the country, whether it was Manchester, Wales, the South, or the Midlands. Our days were spent driving, listening to demos and discovering new bands. It was a remarkable experience, living out my passion for music to the fullest, but it was also frustrating, because scouting was essentially like panhandling or prospecting: you had to sift through a lot of shit before you'd get to the tiny nuggets of gold.

The late '80s and early '90s was a pivotal period in the music industry and it was a time of cultural fusion and change. It was a time when genres were less rigidly defined and the lines between them were often blurred.

Island was at the forefront of the changing British musical landscape, not least because it offered an eclectic alternative to whatever America had to offer. While the Dutch and Germans can bang out some half-decent techno, Italo house can still rock the party, Balearic beats continue to be the playlist staple to many a Mediterranean holiday conception, and Sweden still has, er, ABBA. If the global pop music industry were a race, there'd only be two horses in it: Britain and America. To be clear, this isn't in terms of retail value: Britain consistently lags behind Japan and Germany, while America ultimately always comes out on top. No, what sets Britain and America apart from the also-rans is creative dominance, much of which is built on the fact that both are multicultural societies and kleptomaniacal when it comes to discovering, importing, developing, nurturing, marketing and rewarding artists from anywhere in the world.

British independent labels were in vogue and therefore targets of the big American and multinational record and entertainment corporations. Island Records got bought; A&M got bought; they all got bought, and all because of the quality, richness and originality of songs, sounds, looks and attitude that came with small, quirky or idiosyncratic British labels. At the heart of this, all roads led back to black music. Island subsidiary 4th & B'way Records was essentially a black music label specialising in hip-hop. Then Chrysalis Records had Cooltempo, which was a dance label; Virgin had Circa Records. You also had a host of commercial radio DJs and personalities, such as Trevor Nelson, Matt 'Jam' Lamont and Matt White, who combined DJing with A&R, producing and remixing as labels started to pull these guys in and tap them up for their expertise. It was an exciting, transformative time within the music industry. British artists and musicians were finding their own unique voices and sounds, rather than simply emulating what was happening in the US. This period saw a resurgence of cultural pride and authenticity.

Having previously been overextended financially, Chris Blackwell had given U2 a piece of Island in lieu of outstanding royalties owed to them. But as the band had gone on to be supersuccessful, and generate huge incomes for the label, the company had become way bigger than he had ever imagined. It was thus time to cash in. No sooner had I joined Island than Chris sold it (along with the publishing company, Island Music) to UK-based PolyGram for £180 million. (In 1998, in keeping with the music industry's cannibalistic appetite, PolyGram merged into Universal Music Group after Seagram acquired the company for $10.6 billion.)

What was I getting into?

Chris had founded Island in Jamaica, along with Graeme Goodall and Leslie Kong, originally focusing on Caribbean music and artists. The label's first big hit was 'My Boy Lollipop' by Jamaican teenager Millie Small, which reached number two in the UK in 1964 and number two on the US *Billboard* Hot 100. (In the US, the track was released on the Smash Records label, which was a subsidiary of Mercury Records. Mercury is owned by Universal Music Group, parent company of Island Records.)

In the early '60s, Chris began building the label in his native London, specialising in imported Jamaican music through the likes of Jimmy Cliff and Toots and the Maytals, but also signing UK acts such as John Martyn, Fairport Convention and Free, and later, Roxy Music, King Crimson, Sparks, Traffic, Cat Stevens and Steve Winwood. But perhaps the heart and soul of the label is best embodied by Chris's marquee signing, Bob Marley, whose first album for the label, *Catch a Fire*, was released in April 1973. When the Wailers disbanded the following year, Marley cut a string of classic albums for the label as 'Bob Marley & the Wailers' between 1977 and 1980, including *Exodus*, *Kaya* and *Uprising*.

Following Bob's untimely death in 1981 aged just thirty-six from an acral lentiginous melanoma (the most common form of melanoma found in people of colour), Island could've easily hit the skids, but Chris had another ace in the hole: a young rock band hailing out of Ireland by the name of U2.

As an independent, more artist-focused label, Island had played a crucial role in nurturing the creative drive and artistic freedom of the Bob Marleys and the U2s, while also having the clout to make deals that generated the income. Island and other independent labels had allowed artists the freedom to experiment and create music that was true to their own experiences and backgrounds. As a result, we saw the emergence of diverse musical styles and genres that reflected the multiculturalism of Britain. The 1990s continued to be a dynamic period for black music and culture in the UK.

While the good times rolled there was also a sense of pressure, especially for those from underrepresented backgrounds, to try to make a profound cultural statement or to be seen as a voice of their generation. To 'represent'.

Success in the music industry, as in any field, often requires a focus on both artistic expression *and* business acumen. While making culturally significant music is essential, it's also important to navigate the industry's financial and commercial aspects to sustain a career and achieve longevity. This doesn't mean compromising one's identity or values, but rather finding a balance between creativity and business.

Without sounding preachy, it's crucial for those entering the industry, especially those from diverse backgrounds, to understand that they can contribute to the cultural landscape without solely shouldering the burden of representing an entire generation or community. There are many ways to make an impact.

Ultimately, it's about finding a path that aligns with one's goals and values while recognising that success in the music industry often involves a combination of creativity, strategy and resilience.

In the music industry, it's easier to be defined by your big economic successes because everybody knows about them, rather than the culture that only a few people are aware of. Working for Island, eventually, I was able to use my successes to curate culture. With economic power, you can sign acts that bring something unique and meaningful. You can venture in a different direction. Success allows you to pursue the things you were passionate about before anyone had heard of you. But you need success. And in the music industry, hits are the way we keep score.

5

Ten Commandments

I shall not be the icing on your cake
And I shall not be the candy on your arm
But I shall be seen
And I will be heard!

— the Specials[1]

I'd barely been at Island for two years when I got into a blazing row with my boss, Julian Palmer, over what I hoped would be my first signing as an A&R. I'd had my eye on a band from Manchester called Ashley & Jackson, who were part of an 'industrial funk' movement that included the likes of A Certain Ratio, Public Image Ltd and Cabaret Voltaire.

It was a baking hot summer's day, so perhaps the heat had got to me. As I argued my corner, practically squaring up to Julian, he refused to let me sign the band, so I threw my toys out of the pram and said, 'Fuck it. I'm off, then.'

---

[1] Terry Hall, Lynval Golding, Horace Panter, Torp Larsen and Saffiyah Khan; Island Records.

Hearing the commotion from his office upstairs overlooking the war room, Island MD Marc Marot bounded downstairs.

'What's the problem?' Marc asked, looking me up and down as I eyeballed Julian.

'He won't let me sign an act, so I might as well leave.'

'Okay . . .' Marc strolled over to the exit door, opened it and beckoned me over. 'On you go.'

It was one of those do-or-die face-saving moments. Egos on the line, that sort of thing. No one was backing down, least of all me. So, not for the first time, I walked out the door. Within minutes I could feel the weight of my decision pressing down on me. I'd applied to dozens of record companies and didn't even get the executive middle finger in response from any of them. Yet I had just walked out the door of *the* Island Records, the label with a back catalogue that had soundtracked not just my life, but also my parents' generation. And here I was, flipping the bird to all that. Was I mad? Probably. At the time, however, I felt there was some divine method to my hot-headed madness.

And initially, it seemed as if there was. Luckily, I found a new job easily enough, at Big Life, which had been founded a couple of years earlier by music management gurus Jazz Summers and Tim Parry. They indulged me with my first signing – none other than, of course, Ashley & Jackson, whose 1990 single 'Solid Gold' soared to the dizzy heights of, er, number eighty-nine in the charts.

Nevertheless, Jazz and Tim backed me to the hilt. They became fantastic mentors and the first people in the industry to *really* teach me how to make records. After a stint at Big Life, I then joined Gut Records, which had been founded in 1991, set up by Island's former head of promotions, Guy Holmes, who was trying to follow up on the huge success of Right Said Fred's 'I'm Too Sexy'. Despite its massive success, however, I knew I'd really screwed up. Creatively, this wasn't where I wanted to be.

As luck would have it, ironically, thanks to the success of 'I'm Too Sexy', the phone started going off the hook and one of the calls I got was from my old sparring partner at Island, Julian Palmer, asking me to come back. I made him sweat . . . for all of thirty seconds. Going back to Island was the best career move I ever made. I wouldn't say that I was the finished article by any stretch of the imagination, but during that time away I'd grown up and matured into the role of an A&R.

Now installed as A&R manager at Island's 4th & B'way imprint, the new and improved me set about focusing on signing acts that stood for something, artists such as British-Tunisian singer, actress and artist Hinda Hicks and hardcore British rap outfit Silent Eclipse, whose lead MC was called MCD. The dude had a distinctive, raspy voice and was on that 'conscious' militantly political tip that would reach its zenith in the '90s, a decade that was arguably the golden age of hip-hop. We recorded the LP *Psychological Enslavement* in 1995, which one hip-hop blogger nailed as 'an album full of reality raps and attacks towards the government delivered with a vehemence and intensity that aimed to teach the youth to open their eyes'. I had big plans for the brotha, but it didn't work out and that was the end of that.

Not long after re-joining Island, along with Julian Palmer and Dave Gilmour, we won 'Best A&R Team' at the Music Week Awards. Island allowed me to express myself. I had artists that were selling out the Jazz Cafe in Camden and Subterania in Ladbroke Grove, and I'd been on the cover of *Blues & Soul* magazine, but being the middle-distance runner that I was, I was only just starting to hit my stride. Looking around at the rest of the field, I began to think, *You know what? I can take these clowns.* Having now realised what success looked like from a record company point of view, however, I desperately needed to score some hits.

In the summer of 1994, I got to work with one of my all-time favourite bands, Public Enemy, on their fifth studio album, *Muse Sick-n-Hour Mess Age*, which was released on the seminal hip-hop label, Def Jam. Island used to release all of Def Jam's repertoire in the UK and that meant I had the job of managing remixes for those tracks. For example, I got legendary New York house DJ and producer Todd Terry to remix Montell Jordan's hip-hop anthem, 'This Is How We Do It', and commissioned The Prodigy and the Chemical Brothers to remix a bunch of Method Man's tracks, including 'Bring the Pain' and 'I'll Be There for You/You're All I Need to Get By'.

While Public Enemy were in the UK promoting their new album, I managed to hang out with the band's frontman and figurehead, Chuck D. One of the incredible perks of being at the heart of the global music industry is having the opportunity to collaborate with my musical heroes and the privilege of being in the same room with them. Chuck was someone I grew up with, so to speak, in my bedroom, my sitting room, on the streets, in friends' houses, clubs and pubs and bars via an array of Hi-Fis, Walkmans, ghetto blasters, sound systems and massive rigs at the likes of the Brixton Academy. I listened to his lyrics and music on a loop with passion. When Chuck rapped, I hung on his every word, which I could recount verbatim from every song, record, or album he'd ever made.

When I finally met Chuck in the flesh, however, I made a bit of a dick of myself. I'm cool being in the room with the likes of Bono or Bon Jovi or whoever because it's my business to be around that kind of talent. But there are those rare artists who, as a result of being part of the soundtrack of my youth, still give me goose-bumps when I'm in their company and Chuck D is one of them.

So, there I was, basking in Chuck's reflected glory at Island HQ as he charmed his way through yet another press interview or record company meeting when I'm tasked with taking him to the Forum in Kentish Town, north London, for a soundcheck for that night's gig. Having navigated rush hour, we were about 300 yards away from the venue and just about to turn into the high street when a lorry suddenly slammed on its brakes in front of us and we came to an abrupt stop. Oh, shit: I'd rear-ended the lorry, jolting Chuck backwards then forwards like a crash-test dummy. Dang! It was a nerve-wracking moment, especially since he was just a couple of hours away from performing. Thankfully, Chuck walked away without whiplash, and I walked away without a multi-million-dollar lawsuit, but my dubious claim to fame when it comes to the world of hip-hop is that I had a car crash with Chuck D and didn't get torn a new arsehole – either by Chuck or the label.

That's why, years later, having not heard from Chuck in an age, I came across a tweet he'd put out after he'd watched the documentary, *Keep On Running: 50 Years of Island Records*, which aired just before I'd been made CEO of Island US. 'Just watching the Island documentary,' the tweet read. 'I got to work with that Darcus Beese. He's a formidable cat.' I was like, shit, he remembers me from my early A&R days. I was so proud that he saw me in that light.

Partly because I'm a bit of a loner, but mainly because artists inhabit their own solar system and only ever enter mine when they want or need something, I've learned to keep a healthy distance from the talent. But whether it was ferrying Chuck to a gig or hanging out at Heathrow Airport when he was laid over, as a kid, even doing the 'dirty work' of a junior A&R for my musical heroes was beyond my wildest dreams, and crucially, made me feel like a fan and thus I was able to understand how fans regard their idols. When you've got some of the biggest names in pop on speed dial it's all too easy to become complacent and forget that the relationship between a fan and an artist, like that of a football supporter and their club, or a trainspotter and the *Flying Scotsman* has a deep meaning to that person, no matter how abstract, virtual or irrational it seems to an outsider.

Suffice to say, I have not had such a positive relationship with every artist I've engaged with over the years.

One such example is Lauryn Hill, formerly of the Fugees. I started having conversations with her representatives about doing a deal, which included having some of her demos played down the phone to me. When I went to talk to my UK chairman, David Joseph, about signing her, he told me in no uncertain terms that the label had no interest in putting Lauryn on the roster, not least because she was an American artist and it was rare for us to sign direct with US acts.

When I called Lauryn's management to deliver the message, they were gobsmacked as to why I was giving such a big name the cold shoulder.

'Well, I'm gonna have to take that back to Lauryn. She is NOT going to be happy,' said her manager.

'Yeah, I get it,' I said, making my excuses and hanging up.

Within a matter of minutes, I'm in the kitchen hanging out with Alison, doing the washing up and generally lost in domesticity when my mobile rings. It's Lauryn Hill's manager, again.

'Hey, Darcus. Hold up. I'm just gonna put Lauryn on the phone.'

I'd been completely blindsided.

'So, the white man says, "Jump" and you say, "How high?"' said Lauryn.

Ouch! This time I did get torn a new arsehole as she ripped into me.

'Look Ms Hill, I'm really sorry, but I took this as far as I could and . . .'

'Whatever,' Lauryn said, putting her manager back on the line.

'Yo, I'm just gonna get out of here,' I said and hung up the phone.

It was often the case that artists – both those who were well-established and those who were new on the block – would overestimate their value, pulling power and the costs involved in doing a deal. Usually, an artist would get an advance, which generally they want to go big on, the manager would want 20 per cent of the action and everyone around the artist is in their ear, telling them they deserve a massive deal. So, an artist may do a deal for £300,000, but on top of that you need promo videos, tour support, travel expenses and so on. By the time you've got through an album campaign, the artist is in debt to the tune of between £750,000 and £1 million, so if the release hasn't been a success and it gets to the option period, the label has to ask itself: Do we plough on with the artist or do we drop them? If you've got a record that's flying out of the box, you probably go back to the artist and negotiate, but a 'million-pound deal' is never really that because the artist gets 10–20 per cent on commencement, another payment on delivery of the album and another tranche on release of the record. The entire sum is never spent purely in payments to the artist.

Money, however, isn't everything, even to the biggest stars.

Once, I was hanging out at Lionel Richie's mansion in Beverly Hills, having been dispatched by Universal chairman Lucian Grainge to try and get a record out of him. According to *Architectural Digest*, Lionel's '28-bedroom house was originally built in 1929 by Harry Koerner and William J. Gage for Carrie Guggenheim' and overlooked the ultra-exclusive Los Angeles Country Club. Lionel has sold over 100 million albums globally, has an Oscar and four Grammys and is worth, if the tabloids are anything to go by, an estimated $200 million.

But he's still a black man in America.

Gazing out of a rear window of Lionel's spectacular home, I could see golf balls whizzing by the lush gardens down below, which overlook the fourth hole of the golf course. To stop stray balls from coming onto his property, a high mesh fence had been erected, but some still managed to make their way over the top and into the garden.

'Wow, Lionel,' I said, marvelling at the view. 'Do you play golf on the course?' It was another one of those, 'Are you mad?' moments.

'Hell, no,' Lionel said. 'Black people aren't allowed over there.'

'What? But you back onto the . . .'

'Man, it's the same old, same old. White people have got their golf course. Jewish people have got their golf course . . .'

'And what about black people?' I enquired.

'Brother, black people don't want to build no golf course.'

While America is still mired in structural racism, social segregation and cultural apartheid, Britain also still has much to answer for. Inspired by Mum, Dad, Chuck and a growing black British consciousness to 'fight the power' in my own small way, in the industry, I had started to gain a reputation for having a bit of 'edge'. Our Ashley & Jackson spat never far from our minds, Julian Palmer once lauded me as a 'militant rebellious young firebrand of an A&R man with an encyclopaedic knowledge of gangsta rap' who made a 'defiant stand over a cardigan-wearing Acid Jazz combo'.

One day, I found myself in yet another heated argument with a co-worker. I don't believe it's a situation that's unique to me, but I was reminded of the incident that saw me walk out of Island Records the first time. I could feel my emotions getting the better of me again. I had just come back to work after attending a funeral and, understandably, was feeling a bit raw and emotional. I had also conducted a radio press interview earlier that same day. When I walked into the office, one guy that I didn't particularly get on with thought he could criticise me for how short the interview was. There were some disparaging remarks. I couldn't let that slide. Once again, I had Dad's warning, 'Don't let white people fuck with you,' ringing in my ears. My philosophy has always been that if I ever disrespected someone, I'd apologise and make amends. So, I wasn't about to let people disrespect me either. As he started skulking off upstairs, I went after him and confronted the guy.

'Who do you think you're talking to?'

I remember the look on his face as he realised he had never been in a situation like that before. Before anything could happen, someone stepped in to intervene and thankfully, it didn't escalate further, but I was warned that if it had, there would have been zero tolerance for any physical altercation. What the hell was I doing?!

Considering the musicians and artists I'd come across over the years, many of whom ranged from being a tad eccentric or offbeat at one end of the spectrum to highly combustible and batshit-crazy at the other – *and* having grown up in a volatile environment myself – you'd think I'd be able to read the signs in myself. But I couldn't.

The music industry is chock-full of clichés. You can either wake up in the morning and dive right into those clichés or make a conscious effort to defy every single one of them. But, let's face it, the music industry is no walk in the park. It's this intricate web where power dynamics play out – the labels hold a significant upper hand while artists initially have less sway unless they shoot up into superstar territory. Then it all levels out and artists gain more clout as they keep racking up success.

So, you see, the myths and the underlying mistrust, they've always been there as a fundamental part of the music industry. It's like this constant tug-of-war, creating both tension and attraction. It's what keeps people sharp and on their toes. But, yes, in my case, sometimes that would spill out onto the shopfloor. There aren't many businesses or industries in which you wake up one day and are paid to gamble a massive pile of money – thousands or millions of pounds – on an artist based on a gut feeling or a whim. Imagine waltzing into the bank, asking for a million-pound loan and explaining, 'Well, there's this band I'm eyeing up; I've got a good vibe about them.' The bank manager would probably look at you like you'd grown a second head.

'Hold on, how do I get my investment back?' they'd enquire. 'When will that happen?'

'Um, not sure.'

'And how do you even know you'll get it back?'

'Well, they're just amazing.'

That'd be the quickest way to get thrown out the door by security.

But that's the captivating thing about the music business. We're handed this pot of money and told to go invest it based on our instincts. It's wild when you think about it. So, each day, you're out there, sealing deals, handing over these funds to artists you believe will shine in their chosen lanes. But let's get real, it doesn't always pan out perfectly. And when those times come, and things veer off course, that's when tension spikes, fingers point and blame flies around. When you're riding the wave of success, everyone's high-fiving, all smiles, hugging each other and giving it, 'Woo, woo!' But there have been times when deals fell apart at the last minute, heated arguments ensued, or artists made unexpected demands that seemed impossible to fulfil. It's all part of the territory when you're working with passionate and visionary people in the music industry. But when things swerve a bit left, it's a whole different story. Once blame starts getting assigned or someone gets the hairdryer treatment, that's the time to make sure you're not in the room.

And here's the kicker – out of every hundred things we sign, a whopping ninety-nine of them won't hit the jackpot. So those relationships, the ones that don't pan out as planned, that's where the real daily grind of managing comes in.

There's a considerable amount of trial and error in this game. Signing a chart-topping artist isn't an exact science. Like scouting footballers, there's quite a bit of wastage and write-off in the mix. And the intriguing thing is, if you manage to nail one or two of those decisions, the successes can often overshadow all the losses you've encountered. But the real question is, how many of those do you get? How many can you score in a year versus the number that flop? If someone hands me a substantial amount of money to invest, statistically, I should get it right at least once. It's like a coin flip eventually landing on heads. So, if luck shines your way a couple of times throughout your career, suddenly you're hailed as a genius. But here's the twist – calling someone a genius based on luck over an extended period is a bit of a stretch.

This is where repetition and consistency come into play. It's about measuring success and finding ways to hang your name on what works. You just don't talk about the failures. Unless you're writing a book. When people ask about my credentials, I can proudly point to a whole line-up of achievements. However, there will always be those who only emphasise one or two standout moments because in truth the failures far outweigh the successes. For every Messi or Ronaldo there's a thousand, ten thousand kids who played for their school, district, county, maybe even got a pro contract . . . and then busted out. It's the same with the music business, or any talent-based industry. You're constantly sowing seeds, farming, nurturing, but often your crops just fail and there's nothing you can do about it.

There are so many different metrics to gauge success now. Times change, perspectives shift and how we measure success adapts accordingly. By enduring the various cycles, the music industry has gone through over the past few decades and capitalising on this 'volatility' to become an agent of change (as opposed to just another suit craving for the next hit), I manage to formulate my own secret sauce for being an effective A&R, a record label exec and, dare I say it, thought leader and change maker. Without experiencing season after season of shifts in taste, fashion, looks, culture and, of course, sound, I would've developed

Grandfather Cipriani and Grandmother Lucille on their wedding day.

Beatrice Mae Beese, mother and grandmother.

Left: Saying goodbye to Dad on the way to Phoenix, Arizona.

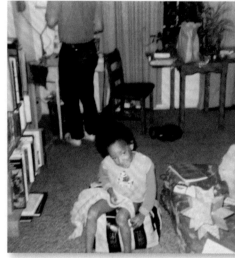

Below: Boy with his blanky in Phoenix, Arizona.

I got royalty and loyalty inside my DNA. © *Paul Trevor*

Above: Out front.

Left: Roleplay time: music manager.

Below: With the mandem at the youth club.

Above: Straight out of Compton (Henry Compton School).

Right: One of the many letters sent home.

Below: Dickhead.

Inner London Education Authority

Henry Compton School

Headmaster: D. E. GREEN
Deputy Headmasters: D. E. A. CHANT
J. R. LEAFE

KINGWOOD ROAD, FULHAM PALACE ROAD
LONDON SW6 6SN
Telephone 01-381 3606/7

14th October, 1981.

Mr. & Mrs. Beese,
41 Tynemouth Street,
London, S.W.6.

Dear Mr. & Mrs. Beese,

Yesterday another serious incident of violence took place in
the playground. Despite repeated warnings, certain boys seem
determined to act in an unacceptably physical fashion.

Darcus was involved in yesterday's incident and he has been issued
with a most stern warning as to his future conduct. If there are
further acts of threatened violence, actual violence, or gang violence
on other pupils it will be necessary to ask you to come to the school
to discuss the issue.

I trust you share my concern and can instil a degree of restraint as
far as Darcus is concerned before someone ends up in hospital with
a serious or permanent injury.

If you wish to discuss this matter would you please contact Darcus's
tutor as she is fully aware of the events leading to this letter.

It would be much appreciated if you could acknowledge receipt of this
letter.

Yours sincerely,

D. A. R. Jones
HEAD OF FIRST YEAR

SUBJECT REPORT

Name _Darcus Beese_   Date _24/5/83_

Subject _English_   Class _S2_

Termwork _good._   Examination result _82% (9TH)_

COMMENTS _If Darcus' ability matched his ego he would be at
University by now. He does have a good writing style but does
not often write enough and has to be pushed to produce homework.
His arrogant behaviour can cause problems within the class at times.
If he just stuck to the task in hand he would be a very capable student;
unfortunately I cannot see this happening._ _M.C. Bahr._

Form master/mistress   Headmaster/mistress

Started at the bottom.

Island family in Paris for Bastille Day, 1989.

Chilling with Chris and his late wife Mary on his island in Nassau.

I do.

Dad's tribe.

With my cousin Amoa, who was brutally murdered in cold blood.

Receiving my OBE from the future King.

Outside the Palace with my proud family.

Above: On the stairs of Kensington and Chelsea Registry Office with family.

Above right: Me and my mother-in-law and aunt-in-law, Val and Sue.

Left: My mum, her brother Sven and sister Pia, united after fifty years.

into just another narrowband, by-the-numbers exec, but what gets me up in the morning is going to work thinking that today might just be the day that I hear something or discover an artist that gives me that rush, that almost incalculable 'fuck, yeah' that a fan gets when they play their favourite band's new release, or they randomly stumble across an unfamiliar tune that they just can't get out of their head. My job is to recreate that sense of awe, wonder and discovery, over and over again, so that when fans listen to one of my signings, they wear the needle out (figuratively speaking) just as I did when I listened to a new Aswad, Specials or Public Enemy record for the first time.

In the early days of my A&R career I learned not to sweat the small stuff and think about the bigger picture, in part because I came from a culture where being an agent of change was a given. This is why I see the 'mystery' of talent spotting as a game of creative chess. While keeping an eye on what's happening on the board, in the moment, you're also looking two, three, four moves ahead because the future is where it's at.

As a progressive thinker, I've always focused on artistry and not celebrity because I play the long game. I've learned how to not only spot talent but sign artists I can actually work with, believe in and help develop into agents of change in their own right. Of course, I've had bad runs, but I try my best not to fixate on my failures or take them too personally because if I'm committed to signing and nurturing *real* talent the potential for success, for a checkmate, is always just one move away. My mantra is: 'Stay on the pitch as long as you can and score. Stay on the pitch, give yourself time, think long term.'

Some things in the industry remain constant, while others have evolved. In the past, you could simply perform a gig and have a direct connection with your fans. Today, it's different. You need to establish multiple touchpoints with your audience. It's essentially the same goal, but the nature of the fan-artist relationship has shifted. This means you must put in more effort to establish and maintain that connection. It's not always about reaching a massive audience. Sometimes, it's just about having the right niche. You don't have to be globally recognised. You can be big in your own little space – like being the talk of your town or creating your own tight-knit online community or fanbase. Back in the day, you'd need A-list celebrities to make an impact but now it's about having artists that resonate with the younger generation and their culture. And it's all about personalisation these days. If you have that touch from an artist, it's gold. And from there, it's just figuring out how to make things work, commercially, on the ground.

Kids can spot inauthenticity from a mile away, and if they sense it, they'll quickly move on to something else. This is where patience and the power of the live experience come into play. It's about capturing that raw emotion that makes people genuinely care and want to come back for more. It all boils down to authenticity. Can kids smell it? Does the audience get it? It's often the younger generation, the kids, who lead the way and set the trends in music. They're the ones who can move the needle and it's essential to pay attention to what captures their attention and resonates with them. When you notice that the needle starts moving, the challenge becomes how to make it move even more; how to amplify that authentic connection.

In the past, having a hit in the charts was the only game in town. The music industry often viewed a record's weekly sales position as the primary indicator of its success. However, the industry landscape and the charts themselves have evolved and many artists and businesses now thrive without necessarily dominating the 'official charts'. Today, both artists and labels can build healthy businesses through various revenue streams and strong brand relationships.

So, defining success in today's music landscape goes beyond just having a chart-topping hit. It involves creating meaning-ful connections with fans, building sustainable revenue streams and fostering a vibrant community around the artist's work. Success, in this context, is about more than just numbers; it's about engagement and impact.

But you also have to take into account all of the challenges, like the competition from gaming, the proliferation of TV, both online and offline. It's a crowded space, so the big question is, how do you make people care? How do you really get them to give a shit? You've got to circle back to the core of it all. Everything changes, but some things remain the same. The landscape keeps shifting, but music still has the power to evoke those emotions. It can take you back to your first heartbreak, your first rave or in my case, your first demo. (If you ever get your hands on Linton Kwesi Johnson's 'It Dread Inna Inglan', listen out for my young voice chanting 'Free George Lino'.) So, what does that connection look like in this new world? It's not just about the song anymore; it's about the song, the entire ecosystem and the brand. When a listener steps into this musical world, why do they decide to stay? It's about creating something that makes people turn up for more than just a song. Songs used to mean so much more because you could only experience them in specific places and buy them in cer-tain ways. To meet an artist, you had to wait for them to come to your town. But now, in the age of live streaming and social media, that gap between artist and fan is almost non-existent. It's like the artist can show up at your doorstep in a matter of seconds. That's a whole new world we're living in.

From ska to rock and folk, Island Records fearlessly embraced a spectrum of genres and artists, with an amazing roster. We established up-and-coming British rock acts like Traffic, Jethro Tull, King Crimson and ELP. And when it came to the softer sounds of the singer-songwriter genre, Island was there to champion artists like Nick Drake, Fairport Convention and Cat Stevens. But the label's impact went much further. It made significant inroads into reggae, becoming a cornerstone for promoting Jamaican artists beyond Bob Marley, such as Burning Spear, Black Uhuru and many more. The label even broadened its horizons to embrace world music, showcasing talents from Africa, including Salif Keita, Ali Farka Touré and King Sunny Adé. One of the most striking aspects of Island Records was its ability to adapt and diversify. It welcomed punk with open arms, introducing the Slits, ventured into experimental sounds with Grace Jones and Tom Waits, and explored electronic beats with the Orb and Talvin Singh.

I couldn't see people being passionate about an Epic or RCA or BMG record or whatever in the way that they could about an Island release. But these days, people are more excited about working with the artist than they are about a label. It's not like the days of Stax or Trojan Records or Tamla Motown – labels that drew artists in and made them want to have a piece of the action just from hearing the name or seeing their logo. Maybe Atlantic or Parlophone are the last surviving major labels to have that mystique, that *je ne sais quoi*. I wanted us to be relevant, not just as a proxy for the artists we signed, but as a label itself, a label with an identity, a heart and a soul. I have a romantic view of Island, maybe too romantic. But just as Island was all about the people who worked at the label – ultimately that is what the artists are drawn to. I used to think of the label as a light to a moth; we drew artists towards us, the flame, and as the record shows, we did it spectacularly.

While it could be challenging for white rock A&R professionals to tap into black music's essence, I had a natural advantage. This became my USP, allowing me to create records from a different vantage point, one that embraced a more soulful perspective.

Growing up in a multicultural society, I was as informed about white music as I was about black music. When I entered the A&R space, my taste was incredibly broad and of course I would sign bands that weren't exactly my forte. When A&R Annie Christiansen, Head of A&R Louis Bloom and the rest of the team put Mumford & Sons under my nose, saying, 'This band is incredible!', I went to see them live . . . and sure, I thought they were good and recognised that the lead singer, Marcus Mumford, had an amazing voice. But I just didn't get it. It was banjos and a stand-up bass. Initially, I didn't think they were going to set the world on fire. After the gig, their manager, Adam Tudhope, came up to me and Ted Cockle, drooling, 'This band is going to be the biggest in the world!' I still didn't fully get it, but you couldn't deny the *love* in the room for that band. It took seeing them a couple of times to say, you know what, let's run with it. I believed in my team's passion and their critical opinion and backed them 100 per cent. They were excited about it, it wasn't an expensive signing, so I let them go and do it. Eighteen months later everyone in the industry was patting me on the back about signing Mumford. But the truth is, I didn't see that one coming, and I'm grateful my team did.

My rapidly expanding career as an A&R exec was shaped by a sense of musical adventure and a genuine passion for the artistry that transcends boundaries. Finally, all the chaos, uncertainty, vulnerability, alienation, self-doubt and insecurity I'd grown up with combined with my vocation to give me meaning. In terms of Maslow's hierarchy of needs, I was heading to the top of the pyramid, but every now and again, I'd find myself slipping, down, down, down . . .

Shortly after my first child, Darcey, was born, I was in a meeting with two white guys, who shall remain nameless. I was pitching for a film soundtrack to the project's producer and its composer. The producer was really posh and spoke with not one, but two plums in his mouth. Anyway, during our conversation, an issue arose.

'Well, Darcus, you see, the only nigger in the woodpile is . . .'

I stood up and growled, 'Who the fuck do you think you are? If you don't leave my office now, I'll knock you out!'

Admittedly, such an approach isn't something they teach you on the Stanford MBA Program. It wasn't a particularly professional way to handle the situation; but, then, how *do* you handle such a situation? Bite your tongue? Smile politely? Pretend it didn't happen? Most of the time, the drip, drip, drip of racism I had to deal with came in the form of gaslighting, a lack of support, or needless or snidey interrogation over an idea I'd suggested that a white colleague wouldn't have to endure. The record industry is an overwhelmingly white, male, middle-class space where micro-aggressions against people like me got a free pass because there wasn't a critical mass of black voices around to stand up and be counted. For this reason, every now and again I felt it was my duty – and in keeping with the struggle

I'd been born into – to double down and hit back a little harder than I would've liked to, to make a point and take a stand.

'I *will* knock you the fuck out,' I repeated to posh boy. 'You need to get the fuck out my office. Now!'

Wherever the line was, posh boy had stepped over it and into the sort of arena that gentlemen of a certain calibre would've once resolved in an unequivocal manner: pistols at twenty paces.

In the lexicon of racist epithets, sayings, songs, tropes and sundry casual bigotry and discrimination I'd come across in my thirty-one years to date, 'nigger in the woodpile' was a sur- prisingly new one on me. Like some bizarre, racist version of *Who Wants to Be a Millionaire?*, I had to phone a friend for an answer to this conundrum. In this case, I chose to get Mum on the blower.

'Mum, what does the expression, "nigger in the woodpile" mean?'

Mum paused for a moment, then laughed. 'What context did you hear *that* in?' she asked.

I explained that it had come up during a meeting I'd just had, and so forth, and Mum started laughing again. She then explained what the expression meant and how it originated in the mid-1800s in the US, and I started to laugh, too. The whole thing was just absurd, but also sad, as it reminded me that no matter how dizzyingly high I could climb, there would always be people who were only ever going to see me as a nigger. Or, maybe even worse still in this case: not see me at all.

When you're in the music industry, it's not just about dealing with the business side of things, it's also about navigating all the personalities and characters around you. It's a real juggling act. A minefield. You try your best to treat everyone equally, but let's be honest, it's impossible to manage each person individually.

There's such a wide range of temperaments and characteristics, and that's just when it comes to the staff.

Then you have the artists themselves, who are usually incredibly creative but also *highly* competitive. A lot of these artists, whether diagnosed or not, tend to have traits that might place them on the spectrum. It's something we're more aware of now, but back in the day, it was often seen as them being difficult or moody, something I could of course relate to given my own behavioural issues at school.

Back then, there wasn't much discussion about these things and you were left to manage the talent without much guidance. A&Rs were essentially groups of people within the record company trying to look after artists who often didn't fully understand themselves. From an HR perspective, it was far from ideal. Looking back, it's remarkable that many of us never received formal training for the diverse roles we undertook. We came of age learning on the fly, developing our 'people skills' through trial and error, sometimes with painful results.

6

Rehab

They tried to make me go to rehab,
But I said, 'No, no, no'
Yes, I've been black, but when I come back,
You'll know, know, know

– Amy Winehouse[1]

In 2002, I signed the Sugababes after they'd been dropped by
London Records following a conflict that led to the departure of
Siobhán Donaghy and the arrival of ex-Atomic Kitten member
Heidi Range. We started to work on their second album and on
22 April of the same year, they released 'Freak Like Me'. It was
an instant, out-of-the-traps hit which changed their, mine and
Island's fortunes. When Chris Blackwell decided to leave, the label
lost some of its identity. We had a momentary loss of direction.
But getting Mutya, Heidi and Keisha on the label was a shot in
the arm. This was Island's second generational wave of success.

---

[1] Amy Winehouse; Island Records.

Regardless of their personal dramas – and there was plenty of that – when the Sugababes put out great records, that dictated absolutely everything. But they were tough to work with. You had three very young, very different, inexperienced band members, all with strong opinions, and there was me, still wet behind the ears and lacking any real micromanagement experience. Every hit song we made together they hated. It was non-stop conflict. They say if you can make it in New York, you can make it anywhere. Well, if you can A&R the Sugababes, you can pretty much A&R anything.

Despite the rows, splits and multiple line-up changes, the Sugababes still managed to produce four platinum-plus albums in quick succession for Island and earn me my stripes in the process. This is when I really came of age as an A&R. Everybody thought that I'd wind up with egg on my face with them, so turning the band around was amazing. I felt validated by getting my first proper number one with the girls. After all the near misses, flops and own goals that I'd had, I could finally throw that imposter syndrome monkey off my back (well, nearly). Thanks to the Sugababes, 'Freak Like Me' became my benchmark and raised the bar in terms of personal – but also label – expectations.

This was followed by a huge success with Keane, at which point the buzz finally returned to the office. I was dealing with Hozier, Annie Lennox, Tinchy Stryder, Mumford & Sons, Ben Howard, Florence + The Machine, Bombay Bicycle Club, PJ Harvey and of course U2 – all incredible 'Island artists', all a joy to work with.

After leaving the Sugababes, Mutya Buena came back to Island in 2007 to record her debut solo album, *Real Girl*. When I heard a demo of the eponymous single from the album, which samples Lenny Kravitz's hit, 'It Ain't Over 'til It's Over', I told my team, 'Mutya's cutting that, and that's it!' It was an infectious, empowering anthem and the perfect comeback record for her as a solo artist.

In the same vein, Gabriella Cilmi's 2008 chart-topping debut, 'Sweet About Me', was an inspirational anthem, which gained massive exposure thanks to being a sync on a Sure underarm deodorant ad. This was at a time when syncs could really sell songs. Thanks to the ad, it became a massive tune that year. While it was number one in Gabriella's native Australia for five weeks, number one in the Netherlands, Norway and top five in around ten other countries, it only got to number six in the UK singles charts. Still, it was the most-played record in the UK in 2009, which goes to show that while a well-crafted pop tune can sell deodorant, a half-decent, well-advertised product can sell an artist, too. Sadly, she didn't blow up the way she should've done after having had such a strong debut. Generally, as an exec, you don't want one-hit wonders, of course. You're always looking to make a second album with any artist you sign, regardless of the first album's success. Take Taio Cruz, for example. His R&B-flavoured debut album flopped, so we went back to the drawing board and came back swinging with a dance/pop album that broke the US. Always know when to pivot for the sake of the greater good.

Having gone from cold to hot, I needed a follow-up success to keep me on a roll while the Sugababes ticked over. The only way to medicate imposter syndrome is by injecting more success into the system; I still had to prove to myself, and the doubters, that even after thirteen years in the business I wasn't somehow fluking it. I also had to show the higher-ups that I wasn't a one-trick pony. Universal Music Group chairman and CEO Sir Lucian Grainge had created a culture at Universal that had no time for complacency. You couldn't spend your time looking in the rear-view mirror. So, as much as the Sugababes were a huge success, it was always, 'What's next?' That sharpened me up for what was to come later in terms of running a record label. But as an A&R person, the failures that I had set me up for the successes. And it wasn't long before an artist came my way that redefined my whole career.

One day, in the autumn of 2002, John Campbell, the manager of producers the Levinson Brothers, dropped into the office to see me.

'Have a listen to this,' he said, handing me a demo cassette. I was about to put it to one side to play later when he insisted.

'Darcus . . .'

I started listening to some of his productions. It was good stuff, but not really what I was looking for at the time. Then – POW! *That* voice. Like nothing I'd heard before.

'Who is *this*?'

'I can't tell you,' John said. 'It's something that we've done for 19 Management, which we have to keep very quiet.'

'For fuck's sake, who is it?'

The manager said he was 'sworn to secrecy' and couldn't tell me who it was. This was ridiculous, and patently an attempt at creating a buzz through the standard music business marketing ruse of mythmaking. This wasn't new. Richard Branson started Virgin Records by selling vinyl from a telephone box in Soho? It never happened. Rod Stewart was discovered busking on the street? Nope. (Maybe even what I'm telling you now is a myth. You'll never know!)

It took me months to find out who it was just by continually asking around. I called 19 Management, but they wouldn't return my telephone calls. Finally, I bumped into Felix Howard, who had been writing with the Sugababes, and he played me some songs that he'd been working on. I recognised the voice and asked him who it was, and he ratted the whole thing out.

'It's some girl called Amy Winehouse.'

Having figured out that Nick Godwin and Nick Shymansky at 19 Management were handling her, but with no one returning my calls still, I blagged a meeting with another artist's manager there, until, by chance, not only did I run into one of the Nicks, but there he was, with 'the voice' herself: the Jewish jazz singer-teenager from Camden and force of nature named Amy Winehouse. It was meant to be. The attitude that the world would soon come to discover was the same attitude I found the moment I set eyes on her sitting on the floor, splayed out like a new-born calf. I was still on the up and learning my craft, but that voice . . . She had the potential to be one of the greatest.

All in all, it took me about six months to find her.

The mystery surrounding Amy only made me more determined to get her signature. I wanted to sign her as soon as I heard her. As soon as my boss, Nick Gatfield, heard her, he agreed, 'Let's get this girl signed!' Industry interest in Amy had been building. Her management, quite rightly, wanted to know that there was support from the top down. She was, after all, still only a teenager. Finally, I got her to come into the office, sing a couple of numbers to the team, and generally let everyone see what she was all about. She was a special, unique talent, so I wanted to show her off and, I suppose, give myself a rare pat on the back. With her voice still reverberating around the Island HQ, I signed her up virtually on the spot. When she came to Island, the buzz around the office lifted again. The label was back. *I* was back.

Amy was a breath of fresh air. She was passionate about jazz. She really *knew* it. Correction: Amy knew music, period. In recent years there had been a backlash against a deluge of reality and factual entertainment-based music TV shows, namely *Pop Idol, Fame Academy, X Factor, Britain's Got Talent* and the like. It had gotten to a stage where audiences and fans were not only bored of recycled, reheated reality TV formats, they'd had enough of the manufactured acts and bands spewed out by these shows. Amy came in the wake of all this.

While 19 Management had been developing her for some two years under their wing, she still hadn't done anything in the studio, although she had written several songs. They had been reputedly paying Amy £250 a week, which was to be deducted from her future earnings.

By the time I'd found her, she'd signed a publishing deal with Guy Moot at EMI and through them she formed a relationship with Salaam Remi, which continued through to the making of the record. She had several songs down, although only a few of them made it on to the album.

And so in early 2003 we released her debut album, *Frank*. Four or five songs from the original demo made it, including, 'I Heard Love Is Blind', 'In My Bed' and 'Take the Box'. As far as marketing was concerned, we made sure it was very organic – your first 20,000 or 30,000 copies must be especially so. Our first ever Amy gig sold out, and those early adoptees of her music were the most important people of the campaign, because that's who we were going to build upon. Having her sing live was always stressful, because she would never sing the same song the same way. No matter what you heard on the record, she would never sing the song that way ever again, and she would never sing the song the same way she sang it the night before.

We knew that if we could reach the first 20,000 buyers, those would be real Amy fans and they would establish her fanbase.

We had phenomenal press, but Amy was a very hard act to programme on radio. We struggled except for Radio 2, who supported her right from the start. That helped us to get the album to where we wanted it to be, Radio 2 listeners being generally the core album buyers.

We didn't have much TV initially either. Before you do, for example, the Michael Parkinson show, the general public hasn't heard of you, but you do one *Parkinson* and it explodes. All of a sudden the whole nation knows who you are. But you have to do that at the right time.

We made a video for the first single, 'Stronger Than Me', which in hindsight we shouldn't have done. No one wanted it. We didn't make a video for the second single. Amy's first performance on *Later* wasn't great. She couldn't live up to the hype. She was nervous. She chose to play guitar, which she could play, but a bit clumsily. If social media was as powerful back then in the early '00s as it is now, she would've got slaughtered. I saw this happen a few years later to Lana Del Rey, when she bombed on *Saturday Night Live* while performing 'Video Games' and 'Blue Jeans'. The Twitter pile-on was so bad that she seldom performs on TV anymore.

With a sold-out tour to support the album, Amy was taking off. From a marketing perspective, we used acts like Norah Jones as a reference point for her. Norah didn't rely on hit singles yet achieved massive sales, so with Amy, at first, we didn't prioritise singles and focused on album sales instead.

When she was nominated for Best British Female Solo Artist and Best British Urban Act at the BRIT Awards in 2004, it was no surprise. We knew she was a major talent. I just didn't think we'd get it so quickly. Like any of the big awards ceremonies, sometimes they get it right and sometimes they don't. In the end, that year, Dido won Best Female Solo Artist and Lemar won Best British Urban Act.

While *Frank* was critically acclaimed, and won her, among other accolades, an Ivor Novello Award, it sold modestly at first. And while waiting for Amy to come up with the follow-up, my other artists such as the Sugababes had gone off-cycle, which meant I was now officially back to being cold again. With this cooling, the self-doubt crept in and, coupled with more changes at the label, I threw a hissy fit. I decided to quit for the second time.

Before I packed my bags, however, Guy Moot called me saying he'd signed Mark Ronson and suggested he meet Amy. She was sceptical at first, but they eventually met and went to New York to collaborate. She introduced him to her favourite tracks and they began writing together. Four weeks later, I visited Mark's SoHo studio to hear what they'd created. The moment they played 'Rehab', I was stunned. 'Rewind it, rewind it!' I hollered, like a big goofy kid. The rest of the album followed soon after.

Later, Amy sent me the track list for *Back to Black* and I called her.

'There's only ten songs on here?'

She said: 'I've written the record, it's ten tracks, that's what it is. Now fuck off.'

Amy always knew what it was.

Back in New York, I heard what Amy and her producer Mark Ronson had been up to. They played four or five songs from the album, putatively titled *Back to Black*. After listening to what Amy had to offer, I only had one thought: 'How the fuck do I withdraw my resignation?'

In some ways, my relationship with Island was like that of a caporegime in the Mafia, or a CIA operative. I could never really leave. Every time I did, they pulled me right back in. In fact, at Island, anyone receiving a serious promotion would be described as having been 'made'. To that end, Island was like a crew, a family, a . . . You get the picture.

Eventually released in 2006, to date, *Back to Black* has sold around 16 million copies globally. But despite her success, or perhaps because of it, Amy's problems with drink and drugs, coupled with being tabloid fodder, didn't make life easy. Trying to control or guide her was a waste of time; she simply wouldn't listen to you if she didn't want to. As they say in the Caribbean, she was 'hard ears'. I know that some of the product managers tried to impose their views on her, but this would only lead to a breach in trust. While some artists need guidance and a direct approach, others, like Amy, thrive when left to their own devices. With her, I learned the value of stepping back.

Come 2005, Amy was hard at it with the boozing, partying and, of course, the drugs, she was also dealing with the fallout from her marriage to Blake Fielder-Civil. Consequently, she just wasn't writing enough material to get her back into the studio and cut a new album. It wasn't that she'd lost her song-writing abilities; she just didn't have the subject matter to write about. She had to live it before she could write it. However, striking a balance between life and art, and the conflicting imitations between the two, were patently getting to her.

Meanwhile, things caught up to me one day when following a major bout of cluster headaches, a friend suggested I come over and try one of their super-strong painkillers. Hours earlier, I had necked a box of Migraleve to no relief, so without thinking I knocked back the pill hoping it would numb the pain. Ultimately, it must've pushed me over the edge because as I was driving home, I went into toxic shock and swerved the car over to the roadside, narrowly averting a crash. I just sat there, shaking, my head feeling like it was being carpet bombed from the inside. I was in such a state that I had to call Alison. I literally didn't know where I was. She took me to hospital where, thanks to decades of research and development since I had first been diagnosed, doctors were able to identify that I was suffering from cluster headaches rather than cluster migraines, which are two separate conditions. Finally, I'd got the right diagnosis, and thus, the right medication, which despite having trypanophobia, or an extreme fear of needles, means I can inject myself using an auto-injector to administer a dose of Sumatripan, along with Verapamil, if I feel an attack coming on. Where once I would get excruciating blowouts that could virtually not be touched by medication, now, as soon as I get an aura, a quick jab with the pen gets me back on track, sooner rather than later.

Looking back, I don't know how I managed to get through all those years of head-banging pain without the right medication. In the early years, it would be Mum who'd find me in the fetal position, crying for help. In later years, it would be Alison, watching over me as I was curled up in a ball in a corner of the room. The nickname 'suicide headache' is no joke. There have been times when the pain has been so terrifying that I've just thought, *why don't I end it now?* Other sufferers I've met over the years have said much the same thing, yet curiously, as far as I'm aware, no one has ever taken their own life as a result of these headaches. Before being diagnosed, I'd go to all manner of lengths just to *make it stop.* I'd put my hands in a sink full of ice to try to get the blood to rush away from my head. I'd try to transfer the pain from my brain to another part of my body through squeezing, biting or pounding my flesh. I'd be unable to sit still and find myself rocking, all the while my face would go so droopy and my eyes water so bad that I'd look like a bloodhound. Anyone trying to touch me would get a sharp, 'Get the fuck away from me.' Then, once the 'season' was over, I'd go into remission and all would be right in my neurological world, for the time being.

Headaches notwithstanding, I was in a good place thanks to Amy's incredible success. In fact, I was now officially HOT again. My name was being bandied about as the man who discovered Amy Winehouse, which of course I have huge difficulty taking credit for, given that her success was a true team effort that involved multiple people over an extended period.

I've never signed someone and said, 'We're going to have a hit!' I've never signed someone and said, 'I'm going to make you famous!' and I've never signed someone and said, 'I'm going to make you filthy rich.' My philosophy has always revolved around genuine talent discovery, organic development and sustainable success, and the artists I sign embody that philosophy. This approach means sometimes waiting longer for success, but it's crucial to maintain a business balance. While some projects take their time to mature, others might quickly gain traction. So, while you're slow-roasting stuff in the AGA, you've got to have something popping off in the microwave. Achieving this balance may well take years of hard graft, but my career choices have always been rooted in the long term and that's served me well. Experience has taught me that forced efforts seldom succeed. Instead, my signings focus on quality music, genuine character and a strong work ethic.

Being in A&R means I'm deeply involved, particularly in the studio. There are times when it's best to let the artist and producer take the lead, especially when they're on the right path, but sometimes it's necessary to roll up your sleeves and get your hands dirty. Working with Amy was smoother in terms of day-to-day A&R compared to say, the Sugababes, who needed a much more hands-on approach.

Investing in an out-and-out pop act is always a risk, but with authentic, organic artists like Amy, even if there's a substantial investment, there's confidence in the road ahead. We were certain of her appeal, not just in America but also all around the world.

Our strategy was straightforward: build upon the existing momentum and take things to the next level with the next album. This approach, however, only holds for artists you believe in and see a future with. In the pop genre, initial chart positions often set the tone for an artist's trajectory.

Seeing Amy's career blossom was one of the proudest moments of my life. Witnessing the tragedy that was to come, however, was one of the saddest.

In late August 2007, Amy was meant to show up at a venue in London to shoot the video to her and Mark Ronson's cover of the Zutons' hit, 'Valerie', but when the appointed time came, she was completely MIA. Consequently, the script had to be completely rejigged on the spot, with the bootlegged footage effect of the video now made to look like Ronson, backed by a group of jazz musicians, having noticed that Amy is missing, invites Amy's female fans (the Winettes) up on stage, one by one, to 'sing' (i.e. mime) along to the song. It totally worked, and if anything added to the Amy Winehouse mythology, but it also demonstrated how volatile and unpredictable she could be.

Come late 2009, I'd heard a couple of song demos from Amy that had absolutely floored me. On the strength of these I'd banked on putting a new album out in 2010. Amy had been writing and recording in fits and starts and had been battling with drug problems and poor health, the result of which meant that a series of comeback gigs scheduled for that May had to be scrapped.

Having taken off to Saint Lucia to convalesce and write and record material for the new album with producer Salaam Remi, who had been instrumental in *Back to Black*'s success, I thought Amy was on the mend. I thought Saint Lucia would've proven to have been the ideal bolt hole. But everywhere Amy went she seemed to get papped in a drunken, incoherent state, falling out of cabs and nightclub doorways, tripping up, stumbling, forgetting her lyrics and basically falling apart in public. Contrary to hackneyed opinion, not all publicity is good publicity.

When it came to Amy, I never had any internal conflict about a white performer smashing it with black music. Even before I showed up, Amy was already being embraced by the creative black community. She was already being patterned up by key people in the black music scene, whether it was putting her on live nights or in record shops. For instance, she did a show in Deal Real records just off Carnaby Street, which was run by Mr Tony Tagoe, which was where all the hip-hop heads used to go. She just showed up with her acoustic guitar and did an impromptu in-store gig and everyone went nuts. The same thing happened at her first show in New York, when I flew over to see her play. At least half the crowd was black. That was a powerful endorsement from the community.

Was she a 'white' voice that showcased black music? Mos def. But Amy was different from your average pop star. She wrote her own music inspired by her own lived experience. Amy was 100 per cent the real deal.

To sell records, black artists have always had to grapple with questions like, 'Can I be my authentic self and still sell records?' or, 'Can I make the music that I want to?' or, 'Does my song need a white artist to sing it for me to achieve success?' The spectre of the 'Great White Hope' always loomed over my shoulder, in part because of Amy's commercial success and cult status. No matter how many talented black artists I signed, the most successful ones often ended up being white, and the one that invariably gets mentioned in the same breath as mine is of course Amy Winehouse.

At that time, in my role as a black man working in mainstream music, I faced a constant dilemma. I went to work every day knowing that despite my love of black music, despite a strong, passionate, visceral connection to it, success for me was predicated on having a white voice showcase that music. Why? Because, in a British context, success in the music is bound up in white bean counters cynically crunching the numbers in the belief that a white audience wants to hear white voices – despite the huge business black American artists generate in the UK. Still, I felt a responsibility both to the industry and to myself, which extended to those in the black community, to 'represent', which meant investing in black artists and black music, even though I knew this path would be challenging and there might be more failures than successes.

Ultimately, I wanted to big-up the successes and quietly bury or at least underplay the failures because confirmation bias runs through the industry like a sewage system. No doubt there were white colleagues or rivals (often the two were indistinguishable) who couldn't wait for me to slip up and sign a black British flop, just to support their own agenda, as race doesn't come into it when a white act fails to live up to expectations. Put another way, the level of jeopardy for white A&Rs signing white acts was lower than what it was for me. Failure for them wasn't a meta-statement about their culture, whereas while I could sign mainstream, white acts and fly under the radar, signing black acts was always a bigger risk – financially, creatively and culturally. White colleagues simply didn't have that added problem to deal with.

Likewise, white A&Rs would have acts that would sell out the Brixton Academy or Wembley Arena, while for me, filling the Jazz Cafe in Camden or Subterania in Ladbroke Grove with my black British acts was often as good as it got. This was largely down to the economies of scale that the American market brings to the table. So, I had to be sharp in terms of my signing strategy, from a cultural and chart perspective.

To be clear about Amy, however: signing her, promoting her and developing her career wasn't some sort of cynical attempt to sell a white girl with a black woman's voice. In fact, in the beginning, I didn't think she was going to blow up into the global superstar she became. As I've said a million times, as much as you believe something is amazing, you've got to convince more than the people in your immediate surroundings that that's the case. And that isn't an exact science. With the help of your team, you must convince the rest of the world of the artist's talent and much of that is a leap of faith. To think that I knew some geeky Jewish white girl from Camden, who was a jazz singer of all things, was going to sell 15 or 20 million records . . . that's all bollocks.

With Amy, the fact that stories were leaked to the tabloids, creating false narratives and painting people as the bad guys, is a testament to how challenging and complex the situation can be when an artist goes off the rails. Managing an artist's career and wellbeing while dealing with these issues is a constant juggling act and it's not always clear-cut.

Other than Amy, I've had friends across the social and cultural spectrum, and within the industry, who've had to go through rehab. It's always a tough and often heart-breaking scenario. And there's only so much you can do as a friend, let alone in a professional capacity, to help or intervene. People often ask me if I knew Amy was doing drugs. Other than seeing the consequences of her behaviour, how would I know? I'm not around my roster 24/7. I'm not their dad. They're not my children. They're mature adults with free will and personal agency. It's a tough situation because no matter what you do, if the person is determined to find drugs, they often will, and Amy was a law unto herself. Besides, our society isn't so open that anyone anywhere, especially with a reputation or status, is going to rack 'em up right in front of you. It doesn't work like that. Drug-taking is a secretive thing, a hidden aspect of their lives, until it becomes too much to manage and it starts affecting their work and the business.

At the time, we tried to keep her in the studio for as long as we could as a way of minimising the time she might spend elsewhere getting into trouble. The struggle was real, and the line between responsibility, intervention and individual choices was incredibly blurred. The question of responsibility is a complex one. Is it solely on the person's shoulders, or do their family, loved ones, creative and business partners have a collective responsibility? Nowadays, it's increasingly viewed as the latter. Our understanding of mental health and substance abuse has evolved, and there's a greater emphasis on supporting artists and addressing these issues as a collective effort to ensure their wellbeing and the success of the business.

But it's a delicate balance between building a trusting relationship with the artist and ensuring that you don't get too close, which might interfere with your ability to make rational decisions and their ability to do what you've signed them to do, which is to make hit records.

These relational dilemmas are nothing new. In the case of Colonel Tom Parker and Elvis Presley, it seemed like the old shyster was pushing the King to self-medicate just to get him on stage so he could make that money to clear his colossal gambling debts. With Elton John, it appeared that he had more control over his drug use. Ultimately, however, the responsibility starts with the individual and their drug habit. If they don't recognise the problem or seek help, you can't force them into it.

There's a strong historical and cultural link between drugs and music. Having watched *Rocket Man*, Elton's drug problems were dealt with in a sensitive, perhaps even sanitised way. I came away from the movie thinking that it was the pressure of fame that led to their respective drug abuse, as opposed to Elton and Elvis both being traumatised people with addictive personalities who sought solace by self-medicating a whole heap of shit, as was the case with, say, Ray Charles, Whitney Houston or Jim Morrison. Many people turned to drugs in the music industry, but looking back, it's clear that some of them might have already had underlying mental health issues or trauma that they were trying to cope with. The drugs and rock 'n' roll lifestyle might have just exacerbated those issues. It's a complex web of factors, and a lot of times, the partying is a way to mask or numb those deeper problems.

Despite my trypanophobia, whenever I visit the dentist, they have to give me some sort of sedative to keep me calm. If I need to have an extraction done, I need a general anaesthetic. There's no way I can bear being awake for that, so in a way I get how the likes of Michael Jackson and Prince got deep into serious, surgery-grade medication – not to get high, but just to numb the pain or get a night's sleep. The music business will happily indulge those who can afford it endless ways of escaping pain, be it physical or mental.

It's fair to say that apart from Amy, I've had other artists over the years who have battled with drink or drug problems, but, again, whose responsibility was it to get them cleaned up? Is it the person who wakes up next to them in their bed? Is it their responsibility? Are their mum and dad responsible? Is it a family responsibility? Is it those who signed said artists and come to work and have a business contract with them? Is it *my* responsibility? Is it their manager's responsibility? Or is it everybody's responsibility? Nowadays, we're all coming to terms with accepting that it's a collective responsibility. The same 'village' it takes to 'raise a child' should be there to support adults, too, in their hour of need.

If there was one thing I was addicted to, it was work. For years, I'd been running at 100 miles an hour. My boss, Lucian, had instilled in me the Universal culture to keep looking forwards, which was basically, 'So, you've sold a million records? Good. What's next?' rather than, 'Oh, you sold a million records, that's fantastic. Why don't you take some time out and celebrate yourself and the people you love?'

This mentality was embodied by Lucian's attitude just after Amy had won five Grammys – that's FIVE Grammys – making her one of only a handful of female artists to have ever done so. I was walking up the stairs at Island HQ and Lucian was just ahead of me.

'Hey, Lucian, whassup?' I asked, having not seen him in a while, and of course expecting some congrats on Amy's historic success.

'What?' Lucian said, matter of fact.

'Er, Amy? Five Grammys?'

'Yeah, good . . . well done . . . carry on.' And with that, he walked off.

In the music business you could never rest on your laurels. No matter how much success you had, you learned how to park it and move on. With this amount of cynical pressure on A&Rs, execs, managers and such to produce results, the buck ultimately stopped with the artists. After all, they were the ones sweating blood and tears, and putting their hearts and souls into their work. All we had to do was sell the shit, which, let's face it, when you're dealing with the crème de la crème of talent wasn't rocket science. Consequently, in some cases, if execs like me could feel the strain, even at the top of their game, imagine the effect of constantly performing such a highwire act on someone as emotionally vulnerable and insecure as Amy?

Then, on 23 July 2011, the call came, Ted Cockle told me Amy was dead. She was twenty-seven years old. The news was earth-shattering. For a long time, I found it hard to listen to her music. I still find it hard. But I feel so proud to have known her. Her passing was a first for me: I'd never had to deal with the loss of an artist I'd worked closely with and cared for so deeply. It's not something you fully comprehend until time has passed and you have the chance to reflect on it.

Amy's death was a shock to the system because she was so cruelly and abruptly taken from us. There's only so much the human body can take over a sustained period and even though she had stopped drinking at the time, the damage had long been done. On paper, the coroner recorded her cause of death as alcohol poisoning. But those of us who knew Amy knew that the booze and the drugs were simply a means to an end. We'll never really know why, but something inside her just wasn't for this world.

It was an awful time. Someone that you'd worked with and knew, passing away so tragically, that was rough. She was a musical genius but, at the heart of it, she was a normal human being who'd had problems from a young age. The pressures of the business from all quarters took their toll and it's good to see the business learn lessons from that. You hear the words 'well-being' and 'duty of care' a lot more now, and that's a good thing.

I worry about the duty of care we owe to artists as much as I worry about the responsibility labels have to their audiences.

If we overly regulate and standardise the creative process, it might stifle creativity and turn it into a bureaucratic, insurance-like endeavour. Is it really my place to hold an artist's hand, moralise and spring interventions on them to curb their behaviour, other than to get them into a studio so they can fulfil their contractual obligations? Likewise, is it my business to police the content in an artist's lyrics on the grounds of taste, decency or moral turpitude? Of course, there are subjects that are beyond the pale that I wouldn't put out on a record, just as there are artists I wouldn't sign if I knew they were involved in illegal or disreputable activities. But there's a fine line between doing the right thing and overregulating, and it's challenging to strike the right balance, especially when you're in a business that's in a wider culture where freedom of expression, free will and personal agency are sacrosanct.

For all the high-minded philosophising, however, Amy's death was awful because she was someone so young and vulnerable. Even though you could see the fragility in her and understand that there's only so much a human body can endure over time, it still hurts that she destroyed herself, and no one could stop her. At times, I've even questioned my right to grieve or feel pain over her death because there are so many others who seem to have more of a right. I was part of the record company during that phase of her life, the part that didn't have a fairy-tale ending. On a professional level, there was guilt. And that guilt trickled down into how I felt as a friend and as a human being.

It's not easy to wrap your head around all these emotions and experiences. Grief can be a very self-centred process in a way. It's a way of acknowledging your own feelings and the significance of what you've lost. But it's also a way of paying tribute to that person or thing in your life. And, tragically, aside from Amy, there were others too. While at Island, we also lost Trevor Grills, from Fishermen's Friends, who died after a tragic accident at a gig. Then there was Tom Parker from the boy band the Wanted, another young artist I had collaborated with. Tom was just thirty-two when he died of a brain tumour. It's heart-breaking. Getting that call never gets any easier.

Some artists may find that certain substances, like sedatives or suppressants, can help calm their racing thoughts and bring their creative minds to a more manageable state. Maybe that was the case with Amy. Did the drink or the drugs drive her creativity? No. Ultimately, they killed her creativity.

Island ultimately reclaimed Amy from a media pile-on that had demonised her for years, with the release in 2015 of the Oscar- and Grammy-winning film, *Amy*. Universal UK chairman and CEO David Joseph said to me that it was important that Amy's legacy be preserved and that people should know the real Amy. People should know the genius that she really was and not just this tabloid pin-up.

That wasn't the Amy we all knew and loved.

7

Dynamite

I throw my hands up in the air sometimes
Saying, 'Ayo, gotta let go!'

– Taio Cruz[1]

Occasionally, you get an artist who you really want to sign, but can't, or you argue your face off to sign, only for them to disappoint you, break your heart, crash and burn, or simply flop. For instance, I've always been into Wiley, the 'Godfather of Grime', but the deal I did with him never worked out. He's entrepreneurial. He's a maverick. I used to sit with him when I was just a scout, hanging out with him and the grime crew, Roll Deep, and other grime heads at the old Island HQ. Wiley's still making music, and beefing with the likes of Stormzy – and the entire Jewish diaspora. While I respect Wiley's contribution to British music culture, and I believe in free speech, actions have

---

[1] Dr. Luke, Max Martin, Benny Blanco, Bonnie McKee; Island Records.

consequences. I would never condone any of the opinions that Wiley has voiced on social media.

Conversely, when you're riding high and think you have the Midas touch, you take evermore (calculated) risks and ignore the 'safe pair of hands' type artists as they can feel *too* safe and uninspiring to make you want to take a proper gamble. After all, nothing succeeds like success! Take Ed Sheeran back in the day. We had him on our radar early. Annie Christensen took me to see him doing a gig somewhere before he had a deal and I was like, 'He's a bit, you know, *pop*.' This is no disrespect to Ed. In fact, we've got a mutual respect, and I'll freely admit I dropped the ball on that one. But anything and everything works with hindsight. At the time, Island saw itself as at the cooler, edgier end of the pop spectrum, yet still selling millions of records, so we felt like we didn't have to play it safe. It's easy to forget that pop music is a broad church. At one end you've got sugary, saccharine one-hit-wonder bubble-gum acts, at the other you've got Björk. Not signing Ed was just one of those things. If we'd have signed him, would we have made the right record? Possibly, possibly not. Everyone has one of those Beatles or J.K. Rowling moments, i.e. the one that got away. You can't sign everything, because, well, you don't know everything, do you? But let's be real: if I hadn't have got lucky or had managed the artists I'd managed and not been successful, letting Ed Sheeran slip through my fingers would've been a sackable offence.

If there are only two types of music – good music and shit music – there are basically two types of record deals: deals where you're going to have me come looking for you if you don't deliver sooner rather than later, or those where I don't come looking for you at all. Mumford did the latter. People who do expensive deals aren't confident in what they have; with a smaller deal, as was the case with Mumford, there's less pressure because you know the return will happen quicker.

Sometimes you get that investment right, but most of the time you get it wrong, because those are the laws of averages that we're dealing with in the record business. I don't know how scientific I am about this, but if you sign three things, one has to work, one won't work and the third one might take time to come to fruition and blow up, or just go belly up. Essentially, you're in a creative casino, rolling dice, flipping cards, laying down chips and hoping your number comes up. (P.S. Always bet on black.)

As an A&R manager, I found myself responsible for artists I didn't always fully understand, musically, or whose backgrounds were unfamiliar territory for me. Signing an artist can be a bit like adopting a rescue dog, which sounds a little crass, but by that I mean it's only after some nurturing and growth that you start to see what their pedigree is. Conversely, you can pay the big bucks for the 'finished article', but this can be equally, if not more, challenging because you can't teach an old dog new tricks, which can result in a purely functional or expedient relationship between the artist and the label. Ultimately, as an A&R, you want a harmonious, synergistic relationship between yourself, the artist and their music, but sometimes you wind up clicking with their art more than their persona.

Dealing with artists is challenging, as it often involves a wide range of personalities, some of whom may be volatile or vulnerable. In many cases, the industry may not have the same level of due diligence or background checks as other fields and it's crucial to navigate this terrain carefully. Managing these dynamics requires a combination of empathy, understanding and professionalism.

So, here are my patented Darcus Beese Ten Commandments for Keeping Your Shit Together in the Music Business:

1. Why? Always ask 'why?' Why sign this act? Why release this song? Why? Why? Why?
2. Tell it like it is. Communicate with authenticity and integrity. It's a two-way conversation so encourage feedback and listen!
3. Be human. Keep your emotional intelligence on high alert and be present for yourself and your people. I have averted many a crisis by acting early and with empathy.
4. Don't let them take the piss. Maintain clear boundaries in your professional relationships, making sure everyone understands the limits of your role and responsibilities. And your patience!
5. I've got you. Put support systems in place, both for yourself and for artists. This can include access to mental health professionals and other support networks.
6. Know your shit. Remember, it's not just about creating that hit record. If your artist starts struggling, you need to spot the signs and be equipped to support them.
7. Keep calm and carry on. Develop strategies for handling crises and draw on the expertise of other teams, including those in HR, press and legal.
8. Change your tune. As the industry evolves, adapt with the times to ensure you remain relevant.
9. Look out for number one. Remember, if you're not of sound mind and body, you will be in no fit state to help anyone else.
10. Be bold, be brave.

You're welcome.

One of the key aspects of managing artists is communication. Having open and honest conversations with them helps build trust and understanding. You have to be approachable and create an environment where artists feel comfortable sharing their thoughts and concerns with you, which is why spending quality time in the studio, and actually paying attention to the creative process and not just the end product, is key.

As A&R professionals, we're entrusted by labels to invest in artists we believe in and this can be both exciting and nerve-wracking. Making those decisions on who to sign and invest in is a mix of art and (inexact) science, relying on experience, market trends and a certain level of intuition. But even with all that, there's always a degree of unpredictability and not every venture will turn out to be successful. For every *Legend* by Bob Marley there are a thousand unheralded, unwanted, unloved solo albums out there. As former EMI owner Guy Hands once said, 'Roughly 85 per cent of what EMI does get to release never makes a profit, in part because of the cash spent signing bands and partly due to ill-made bets on the number of CDs the market requires for particular acts.' Guy should know: in 2008, EMI Records signing Robbie Williams, who the label bagged for a cool £80 million, saw over one million unsold copies of his album *Rudebox* sent to China to be crushed and recycled for road surfacing. Years later, Guy lost €200 million when EMI collapsed. Small beer when you consider that the global music industry raked in over $31 billion in 2022.

When things go well, it's a moment of celebration and everyone is patting each other on the back, high-fiving and thinking they're a master of the universe. But when things don't go as planned, that's when the tension and finger-pointing can arise. The music industry is no stranger to successes and failures, so managing relationships through the ups and downs is an essential part of the job, as no one wants to be the last one in the room when a catastrophic decision is made.

I've always been mindful of the weight that signing an artist carries – for label and artist alike. It's not just a business transaction, it's a commitment to someone's dream and vision. You have those conversations, sometimes in passing and sometimes directly, where you explain your vision, your goals, and what you believe in. But, then, there are times when things don't work out as planned and you must make the difficult decision to part ways with an artist.

For a cynical A&R exec, an artist is just another signature on a dotted line, a deal, a bonus; but for the artist, it might be their one big shot at success. I'm acutely aware of that, and I never take it lightly. It can be a tough and even a heart-breaking process letting someone go or seeing them fail on your watch, knowing the impact it has on someone's career and dreams, and maybe even the ripple effect it'll have on those around them.

The music industry can be brutal. These days, there's a growing awareness of the responsibilities that labels and industry professionals have towards artists, both when signing and parting ways with them. Many labels are starting to understand the importance of providing resources and support. I wish the same could be same for the A&Rs, execs and managers I've seen burnt out over the years.

Sometimes you have a great song, but you're not sure how to produce it, and other times you have a direction for production, but no killer song. It's all about finding that perfect balance and making it work. For most of my career I've embraced mistakes and not been afraid to take risks, even if it meant getting laughed at or having my opinions challenged. This attitude of pushing forward despite the fear of failure is an important aspect of personal growth and success. You have to develop resilience, a reptilian skin that allows you to move beyond potential setbacks and focus on the bigger picture. It's an approach that can lead to valuable learning experiences and ultimately contribute to your achievements, but it can also lead to stubbornness, dogma and conservatism, if you're not careful. Undoubtedly, acknowledging how much you don't know, even amid success, is a sign of humility and a willingness to continue learning. It keeps the curiosity alive and ensures you're open to new perspectives and ideas.

When it comes to doing deals with artists, whether it's signing them or letting them go, I've become more of an arm-around-the-shoulder kinda guy than an Alan Sugar, 'You're fired!' type. I tried that approach once, but it just gave off a really bad energy, a bitterness, an anger. Sometimes, off the back of that aggressive approach, karma can get you. If you kick people on the way up, you'd better watch your arse on the way down. I'm not a particularly religious person, but as Jesus says in the Good Book, 'Do unto others as you would have them do unto you.' I've always aimed to take people to one side and have an honest conversation about their future, their strengths, their weaknesses, whether it's for career development with the label, or it's time for them to move on. Everyone I've had conversations with, for good or for ill, has always gone from strength to strength.

Many people – good, bad, and utterly useless – find themselves in leadership positions, managing companies, departments, or even successful artists. While I'm not claiming that my conversations with them were the sole catalysts for their success, it's heartening to believe that positive interactions can leave a lasting impression. What matters is how people perceive and remember you after interactions. Do they view you with respect? Or, in the case of that 'nigger in the woodpile' eedjat, do they remember you as someone who takes no prisoners? It all boils down to what one desires from their professional and personal relationships. If the goal is merely to be perceived as a good human being, what does that entail? It's almost impossible to always embody that ideal, but at the very least, one should strive to be decent and genuine.

When you look at the roster of artists we had at Island, the whole blueprint was built on the idea that the artist and their art should always come first. The success of the label was directly tied to the success of the artists we worked with. I never wanted to take credit for inventing the thing. It was our collective success that gave us power, the power to curate some incredible music, and I never forgot that it's the artists who are the true stars. At Island we never tried to overshadow them. Sometimes, it could catch you off guard and you'd need a reality check to remember that you're not bigger than the artists. You were there to support them.

Once you get into a cycle of success, it's like a magnet. People just want to be a part of it, and it keeps the momentum going. At that point it's all about riding that wave. When you're on it, you seize the opportunity, strategise and do everything to keep it going. Momentum just begets more momentum, and success leads to more success. And when you get it wrong, you pretend it never happened and move the fuck on.

At some point, however, we all have to face up to defeat.

8

To Be Young, Gifted and Black

There's a million boys and girls
Who are young, gifted and black
And that's a fact

– Nina Simone[1]

In late 2005, Dad fronted a documentary on Channel 4 called *Son of Mine*, featuring himself and my younger half-brother, Amiri. Originally, the film was meant to be about Amiri's struggles with the law. Aged twenty, he had gotten into trouble over some stolen passports and narrowly escaped jail. But the director changed tack and the film turned into a portrait of Dad's relationship with Amiri, my father's sixth child. It thus interrogated his questionable relationship and parenting history, something Dad wasn't too keen on exploring in detail, which led to him describing the film as 'crap'.

---

[1] Nina Simone and Weldon Irvine; RCA.

By this stage, Dad had been writing, broadcasting and campaigning for the better part of forty years. He had a serious track record and had established himself as a preeminent voice of Britain's black community. With a weekly column in the left-wing current affairs magazine *New Statesman*, a slate of provocative documentary films aside from *Son of Mine*, such as *White Tribe* and *Who You Callin' a Nigger?*, as well as regular appearances on TV and radio, which would often find him in heated confrontations with presenters or other guests, Dad solidified his reputation as a radical, public intellectual who wasn't to be trifled with – something that made him bankable in the antagonistic British media but which I could see was taking its toll on his health. On screen and, more importantly, in the flesh, despite his bravura, he looked tired and run-down.

Then came the news no one wants to hear: in April 2007, he was diagnosed with advanced prostate cancer. Doing what he did best, he turned his personal travails into a public debate. With typical candour he wrote about his diagnosis and treatment in the *Guardian*:

> Formalities over, he [the consultant] drew the curtain and with a gloved finger penetrated my rectum. The cancer was there. Beads of perspiration dripped from my head and face. My entire body shook uncontrollably. Cancer to me meant death; Mrs Howe wiped my troubled brow. I sat gazing into the middle distance, my emotions shifting from one extreme to the next. I thought of my children and my grandchildren, guilt-ridden that I had imposed so much worry upon them.

I was in a state of shock when I got the news. Shock and resignation. Dad's cancer was aggressive. Fortunately, he ended up having the cancer taken out before it spread to other parts of his body. Yet six months later came an intense course of radio-therapy followed by hormone treatment. I admired his honesty, and bravery, in the face of a disease that he patently feared. Nevertheless, he continued to fight the good fight, writing about his condition and making a documentary about it, both of which he used to raise awareness among men of African-Caribbean descent, who, nobody really knows why, are three times more likely in the UK to die of prostate cancer than white men.

From the time I turned forty, I'd sprung a leak. Not only was my father's mortality under the microscope, but I started to question my own mortality, too. After his illness came to light (by chance, from being treated for type 2 diabetes), I then started having stomach problems, so, at Dad's prompting, I went to see my doctor. Some rudimentary tests revealed that I was suffering from nothing more than a case of bad indiges-tion, but nevertheless he also did some blood tests. When the results came back, I discovered, much to my concern, that my own PSA (or prostate specific antigen – the protein that healthy prostates produce in small amounts) levels were higher than normal. After my doctor asked if there was any history of prostate cancer in the family, and I told him about Dad, he suggested that I get checked – a standard precaution for men over forty-five.

Days later, I was sat in my local surgery, pants round my ankles, behind a curtain in a consulting room.

'Right, I'm going to have to do the finger-up-the-bum test now,' the doctor said, trying to make light of what is, for many men, the combination of two of our greatest fears: the prospect of cancer and the prospect of a finger up the bum.

I bit my lip and felt a gentle massaging of the prostate, which thankfully only took a matter of seconds. I gave the doctor a urine sample, but that wasn't the end of it. The urine test flagged up a potential problem. Now, he wanted to check me in for biopsies, which needed to be taken from the piece of skin between your asshole and your balls. The scientific term for this sensitive stretch of flesh is the perineum. They wound up targeting thirty-two different injection sites in that small area – thirty-two biopsies – which meant me having a general anaesthetic.

A nurse had told me that after waking up I might pass a little blood. As I came around, groggy from the anaesthetic, I couldn't see anything or feel my legs. I could feel my head, but I could not feel my asshole. It felt like I didn't *have* an asshole. As my faculties slowly returned, I went to the toilet. The nurse wasn't wrong: it wasn't like there was blood in my urine, I just started pissing blood. I was shocked and scared. It was one of the most traumatic moments I'd ever experienced. Fortunately, the biopsies revealed that I was precancerous; but from then on I would have to monitor my condition with annual MRI scans. It was a significant wake-up call, and I can't stress enough the importance of getting checked, even if you're not over the recommended testing age of forty-five. When you factor in the disproportionately high rates of diabetes and hypertension among people of African descent, prostate cancer is yet another timebomb the black community has to defuse.

* * *

In the summer of 2008, I was made co-president of Island along with Ted Cockle, who had come up through the ranks to become head of marketing, having moulded, shaped and developed the careers of artists that included Mumford & Sons and Florence + The Machine, two groups that have gone on to global acclaim. When I took over Island with Ted, I wasn't taking over a pop label; I was taking over a cultural icon – an establishment, even.

My thing was like, what would the managers of all the acts that *aren't* black now be thinking about me taking over the reins with Ted? Was the chairman going to get quietly lobbied? Would secret haters be whispering in his ear, all Machiavellian, 'Are you *really* sure that Darcus is going to co-president this with Ted Cockle?' Maybe he did get lobbied . . . but I never found out about it. Again, I had cause to be proud of that roster because it was genuinely diverse. And it showed that I could curate an eclectic array of serious music, that I could sit in a room with Giggs or Bono or Amy or Shawn Mendes and not be scared or intimidated by pop-star egos.

Getting the co-presidency, I felt like I was finally curing myself of the dreaded imposter syndrome I'd had ever since school. Tracing my A&R development from the early days of signing Hinda Hicks and Me One to later signings such as Taio Cruz, Amy Winehouse, Jessie J and John Newman, my track record demonstrated, through these artists, that I brought something unique to the table. My involvement in these artists' careers not only helped shape my A&R perspective, but they also helped maintain Island's unique identity. John Newman's 'Love Me Again', for example, wasn't only an amazing Northern Soul-inspired floor-filler; it gave rise to a promo video that has now passed one billion views on YouTube. The track is also the signature tune on the epic football video game FIFA 14. To be part of something with that sort of global multimedia reach, and pop cultural impact, just teaches you to develop a big-picture perspective.

Meanwhile, Jessie J was very much a product of the online era. A year before I came along, most of the material that wound up on her 2011 debut album, *Who You Are*, had existed online. Whether she was singing in her front room or in a rehearsal or at a gig, all her stuff was out there. Jessie totally embraced the digital age and exemplified it.

While we were riding high at Island, away from the bubble that is the music industry, reality was hitting hard on Britain's streets. On 6 August 2011, the UK erupted in flames as a result of uprisings that had been sparked by the police shooting of a young black man named Mark Duggan in Tottenham, north london.

In an attempt to bring some understanding and context to this dark chapter of modern British history, Dad appeared as an interviewee on the BBC. He'd spent decades being invited onto such shows as a representative voice of Britain's black community, so he knew how to handle himself. This occasion was no different. Despite his age, Dad was still a formidable character on screen. Introduced, bizarrely, as 'Marcus Dowe' by the presenter, the live on-air exchange between the two was incendiary. Standing on the street in Croydon, and set against the backdrop of the London Fire Brigade battling to put out a burning building, Dad's confrontation with the white, female presenter illustrated the chasm that existed between the mainstream media and those still fighting for representation. After nearly four minutes of sparring, in which Dad rebuked the presenter with, 'I don't call it rioting, I call it an insurrection of the masses of the people,' she sought to have the last word with a knockout blow.

'Mr Howe . . . you are not a stranger to riots yourself, I understand, are you? You have taken part in them yourself.'

'I have never taken part in a single riot. I've been on demonstrations that ended up in a conflict. And have some respect for an old West Indian Negro and stop accusing me of being a rioter. Because you won't tickle me to get abusive. You just sound idiotic – have some respect.'

The BBC later apologised for any offence the interview caused and said 'it had not intended to show [Dad] any disrespect'.

*   *   *

In March 2013, Ted Cockle left Island to head up Virgin EMI, leaving me as sole president of Island. Despite our ups and downs, Ted had been the yin to my yang. If I was the dreamer, he was the catcher. The two of us together, supported by a great team, had smashed it. We had an unparalleled roster of artists that ranged from Drake to PJ Harvey and even Will Young. Suddenly, though, Ted was gone. Without stabilisers, could I ride this sucker on my own? Again, even if imposter syndrome means you're having a crisis of confidence internally, you've got to show outwardly to the people you're leading that everything's going to be okay. If there was one thing I was confident about, it was blagging. Far from being ashamed of this, however, I had learned to embrace it – after all, the British establishment, from colonial kleptomaniacs to one prime minister after another, routinely rewarded people for their ability to bullshit.

Another day, another dollar. One morning, before heading up to my office, I did the customary thing of popping down to the post room to check my mail. It was one of those little things I like to do myself. Flicking through a pile of mail shots, subscription renewals, demos and begging letters, I came across an inconspicuous letter with no stamp on it. This was weird. Was it fan mail? Hate mail? A writ? A bill? Now, I'm no different from most people in that whenever I get a bill, or anything official-looking, I look at it with trepidation, open it up, gradually, maybe just at the corner to sneak a peek or double-check what's inside before ripping it apart and binning it. But when I saw the words '10 Downing Street' and then 'Prime Minister', I tore it open. It read:

Dear Mr Beese,

The Prime Minister's Office would like to put your name forward for the New Year's Honours list and would like to award you with an OBE.

What? The Prime Minister would like to put my name forward for what?! As the letter was printed on cheap, shitty paper, I thought it must be some sort of wind-up. And because the communiqué had come to my office, I thought I ought to have a word with HR, just to clue them up.

'Read this,' I said to my colleague. 'Is someone taking the piss?'

I scanned her face for a reaction as she read the letter, her eyebrows going up and down.

'What? They're offering you an OBE for services to the music industry?!'

On the one hand, I was on a high for having been recognised in such a way. On the other, all those images of fawning establishment toadies and creeps like Jimmy Savile holding up their medals outside Buckingham Palace made my stomach turn. I was worried that Mum and Dad would think I'd sold out. But

Dad was as contrary as ever. If anything, his validation made accepting the gong, well, acceptable. Here was a man who had railed against the system, the establishment and imperialism all his life. But then he hit me with a statement that was irrefutable. 'Darcus, most people who are awarded OBEs are cunts. You are not a cunt. Go pick up your OBE.'

On the day that Dad, Mum and I went to Buckingham Palace to receive the award, he was in tears. Seeing me get the OBE meant a lot to him. It didn't matter that he was anti-establishment. For all of the shit that he had fought for, there was his son, a black man, running a multi-million-pound record company receiving an OBE in Buckingham Palace. At that moment, everything else fell away and he was just a proud dad. That, for me, was the icing on the cake.

Receiving the OBE made me think about the ways in which awards and similar types of recognition are utilised as tools of 'soft power' – something the British are very good at doing, particularly in an international diplomacy context. Soft power is the ability to shape the preferences of others through appeal and attraction, or co-opting, rather than through coercion. By promoting certain cultural aspects, like art and music, governments can subtly convey their values and ideologies. The US, too, is no stranger to using the arts as leverage. The CIA's sponsorship of expressionism and jazz during the Cold War is a prime example. By promoting these art forms, the US was essentially showcasing the freedom of expression and creativity inherent in its brand of democratic society, juxtaposing itself with the perceived rigidity and uniformity of communist regimes.

While representing music business interests through the British Phonographic Industry, I had been in a room with

David Cameron, so, evidently, he'd liked the cut of my gib and seen the potential for a soft power move. Perhaps his government, in recognising and celebrating individuals from diverse backgrounds, was trying to make a statement about the Tories' newfound openness and inclusivity in an attempt to shed off its image as the 'nasty party'.

Considering my background – where I've come from, Dad's radical and angry revolutionary days as well as Mum's challenges – I've taken the road less travelled. As you grow older, you start seeing the world through a different lens. In my own small way, I was becoming more chilled, more spiritual, more empathetic and more giving. Maybe we all, eventually, find ourselves at the other side of the spectrum, far removed from where we once were, but never completely free of pent-up rage and anger.

I've always harboured a slightly utopian view of the world. I grew up in a community made up of all races and classes – that was my reality. Deep down, I think I've always wanted to live in a world that is one big rainbow coalition. You know, when people talk about maintaining the race, I'm like, *Yeah, really?* Everything ebbs and flows. You drop another colour back into the gene pool and it goes black again. So, what was once light-skinned and almost white, you drop a bit of ink in and it goes back the other way. I was never a black separatist when it came to race politics, even though I've been radical to some extent. I am pro-black, but I love everybody. I'm up for a rainbow nation. What will the world look like in another thirty, forty, fifty years? Let's hope for a more harmonious future.

While it's essential to protest and make our voices heard, we also hope that the next generation will carry the torch, understanding their rights and the importance of standing up for them.

As time goes by, our perspectives change, shaped by age and responsibilities. It's a balance between trying not to be selfish, while also considering personal wellbeing as we age. Ultimately, however, what's the point if we don't acknowledge and respect the sacrifices made by those before us, like my parents and the concerns they had?

Being young and angry is natural. It's all right to feel that way when you're young. Letting that anger consume you, though, can be detrimental to your health. My father was also young and angry, but he had mentors like C.L.R. James, who gave him a mature perspective on life as, like many West Indians of his generation, they were cast adrift in Britain as young people, having left their parents behind in the Caribbean. Being young and angry has its place, but there also needs to be guidance. I hope that we can be the guiding, mature voices for the next generation. It's not about standing still or staying in one place. While there has been progress, much still needs to be done. But I don't want to remain stagnant. I don't want to have the same conversations rooted in the same anger. I desire progress for my children, reaping the benefits of the life and efforts I've put in.

It was hard to imagine two artists as different as PJ Harvey and Ariana Grande, yet here I was overseeing a label with a transatlantic roster that was second to none. Whether it was American repertoire or domestic, I was deep in the game. Polly Harvey had signed to Island within a month of me joining the label, and to score a number one with her was, as the kids say, 'pretty lit'. I also found the time in my busy schedule to fly to Jamaica to sign Grammy-winning reggae star Sean Paul, one of the most consistently successful and best-loved artists across any genre. Getting the multi-platinum-selling artist to sign was a coup, as he was one of the biggest hit-makers in the game and a proper Island Records artist. He was one that I couldn't stand by and idly watch go elsewhere.

While it's easy to think that someone who spends their time receiving assorted gongs and signing deals on Caribbean beaches with the likes of Sean Paul is super-confident, truth be known, I'm nowhere near as confident as people think I am. I can walk into a room and exude confidence, even when I don't know what the hell is going on, because deep down I know most people are blagging it as much – if not more – than I am, especially if they work in any form of mass media or communications. It's all blag, puff – it's all about 'the narrative'. But I guess being able to act confident when you're not confident is a display of supreme confidence. Or is that too meta? Suffice it to say, I'm a hybrid, an introvert–extrovert. Whenever I tell people that deep down I'm quite shy, they don't believe me, but I'd rather not be in a room full of people. I'm always the one standing by the fire exit. I'll always take the aisle seat. I'll always get the hell out sooner rather than later. You'll turn around and wonder, 'Where's Darcus?', and I'll have gone home. Again, people think that I like the limelight, but I don't. I like my own company. I'm probably not that social despite, ironically, working in a social industry.

I believe that one of the elements of coolness is vulnerability, combined with a lot of self-contradiction. For instance, you might find someone comfortable in large crowds, like a football match with 50,000 people, yet uncomfortable in a room with just twenty people who are all focused on them. Well, I'd sooner swerve both. In my case, I don't feel any more comfortable in large crowds than in smaller gatherings, or vice versa. My wife and kids can vouch for that. In fact, my son dislikes going to football matches with me because I tend to leave early. Come half-time, I'm gone. I'm not a recluse, but I can easily be reclusive. I don't know what that stems from, whether it's to do with my upbringing. Perhaps being raised as an only child meant I was always okay with my own company and thus became a bit of a loner.

For all the accolades, awards, press interviews and press fleshing, I was still the kid at the back of the group or on the edge of the frame in the photo. Not for the first time, I could feel myself sliding along the spectrum. At one awards ceremony, for instance, pretending to take a call on my mobile, I made my excuses, slipped outside the venue, then walked around the corner, hailed a taxi and fucked off home. Sometimes dropping the shoulder is as important as having a shoulder to cry on.

9

Papa Don't Take No Mess

Papa is the man who can understand
How a man has to do whatever he can

— James Brown[1]

The news came on 1 April 2017.

After seventy-four years of fighting mortality, nearly sixty years of fighting the power, and a decade of fighting cancer, Dad was gone.

The funeral cortège had set off from Brixton and the site of Dad's former magazine, *Race Today*, snaking its way through London to the service at All Saints' Church, Notting Hill, Dad's old stomping ground and the battlefield on which he'd earned his stripes. The floral tributes in the hearse read, 'Papa', 'Darcus' and 'Renegade', as well as a 'D'-shaped wreath fashioned from white chrysanthemums and red carnations. Hundreds of people packed the church. It was standing room only.

---

[1] James Brown, Fred Wesley, John Starks, Charles Bobbit; Polydor.

Walking in and out of the church, one of eight pallbearers, I could feel the weight of my father literally on my shoulders, and the weight of expectation on my mind. By this point, the streets were gridlocked as the Mangrove Steel Band led the procession in honour of my father, Leighton Rhett Radford 'Darcus' Howe, making the short journey up the Grove to West London Crematorium on Harrow Road. Later, the reception was held at the Tabernacle, a landmark community centre for the black and multicultural Notting Hill just a stone's throw away from my Island hub. Here, Linton Kwesi Johnson's 'Man Free (For Darcus Howe)' rang out once more; there was a minute's silence held by an endless sea of bodies; old Black Panthers paid their respects; Black Power salutes punched the air.

Dad's old friend and pioneering Labour MP Diane Abbott described him as 'a fearless, outspoken and witty man with a pleasingly mischievous streak'. *The Times*, that most establishment of papers, opined 'Darcus Howe hated injustice, and he loved a fight', while also observing that to some he was 'nothing more than a rabble-rousing troublemaker, albeit an eloquent and cultured one.'

My eldest sister, Tamara, who herself has risen to the dizzy heights of the British media, said Dad would 'watch and delight in the strength of his DNA – a receding hairline, the Howe forehead, the bandy legs, and naturally, he was all too happy to take credit for our achievements. But in quieter moments of reflection, he also acknowledged the disproportionate contribution of our mothers – strong, intelligent and resourceful women who have also shaped who we are today.'

But perhaps the best eulogy came from Dad himself, on the back of the day's order of service:

I see streets lined with hundreds of citizens, immersed in critical discussion. A thousand Platos in every neighbourhood. We will return to the art of discourse, not the jargon-fuelled rhetoric of the modern-day politician, designed solely to keep us disengaged and baffled. No. A genuine political vernacular accessible to all. The building blocks of a new form of localised, popular democracy premised on equality of ideas. We think, therefore we are.

When an elderly grandparent passes away after being ill for some time or having got to a ripe old age, as much as you're surprised or shocked you can take it in your stride. You're generationally detached enough to process the hurt or pain or loss in a way that helps you to reflect positively on the life they had, and hopefully, the relationship you had with them in a way that doesn't become lost in grief and sorrow. We all know that no one is going to live forever; or you might think that everybody's going to live forever until suddenly, they're gone. But when you lose a parent, you lose your anchor to this world. Regardless of your relationship, your parents are the portal you travel through to get here, to land on Earth. With Dad gone, it was like part of me was gone, too.

Dad was one of the most polarising forces in the race relations movement in the UK, especially for people of Caribbean descent. He campaigned for black rights in the UK for more than fifty years. He was culturally significant, even more so, in his passing. He had all the status, but not the dough. Well, he did have dough at one point, but then he just pissed it all away.

I grew up with people seeing Dad as this larger-than-life character and admiring him for what he was doing. In the same vein, I was like, 'Wow, Dad is famous or important.' So, I was influenced by that. In recent times, however, I've come to realise just how inspirational Mum has been. When you look back at Mum and Dad's CVs, which the Oscar-winning director Steve McQueen pays homage to in his 'Small Axe' film *Mangrove*, you see how people perceive her and that iconic picture of her with the pig's head. It's a representation of what standing up for yourself looks like. But as is so often the case, Dad got all the props, because men have a habit of hogging the limelight.

At Dad's funeral, one particular tune from his life's soundtrack hit me, hard. Music is often associated with the best of times, but it recalls the worst of times, too. As someone once said to me, 'Music occupies a space that isn't really there.' Taken literally, this sounds like utter bollocks, but read poetically, it makes absolute sense. But I digress. The tune in question was one of the Mangrove Steel Band's pan march songs from the late '70s, early '80s. One night during the Notting Carnival, which is every August Bank Holiday, the tune was playing in the house when – BANG! BOOM! CRASH! – it kicked right off between Mum and Dad. Every time I hear it doesn't take me back to Carnival, to painted faces, laughter and the spicy smell of West Indian food wafting through the streets of Ladbroke Grove. No, it takes me back to a scared, powerless, innocent little boy crying in a corner while the two people he trusted the most, needed the most, loved the most, smashed themselves into tiny little pieces, emotionally, spiritually and physically.

I've learned that I need to celebrate and honour my mum just as much as Dad and avoid the pitfalls of letting his relatively more 'spectacular' achievements overshadow her own. It's essential to give her the recognition and appreciation she deserves. Quite often, there's a tension within black communities around black women feeling that they're doing a lot of the heavy lifting and not getting the credit they're due. Many black women were somewhat disconnected or secondary in the frontline battle. When the protests got intense, they were often in the background, and understandably so, at times, given the level of violence between protestors and police. When people think of the revolutionary female aesthetic of that era, they think of iconic figures like Angela Davis – big 'fro, raised Black Power fist, polo-neck sweater, maybe a Che Guevara beret thrown in for good measure. But there were many women who, like my mum, were equally instrumental but were unsung heroes because they were either less interested in, or less able to work, the media angle.

It's astonishing how many people were familiar with Dad's legacy but were unaware of Mum's contribution to the struggle. Yet, when she finally started getting the spotlight through interviews, it was an eye-opener for many. I encouraged her to step forward and share her story because it was essential to highlight that it wasn't just the men who played pivotal roles. There were remarkable women, like my mum, who also made significant impacts. Sadly, many from that generation are no longer with us, and so it's vital to document their stories before they fade.

Thankfully, Dad had the chance to pen his experiences before he passed away. I've urged Mum to do the same, especially when others are apt to take artistic liberties with a story as powerful as the black British civil rights movement. As critically acclaimed as it was, even *Mangrove* sometimes missed the mark.

I've always felt a tremendous responsibility to uphold the legacy. I didn't want to be the one to drop the ball and set things back, making it challenging for the next generation. Success was crucial, not just for me but for what it represented. Demonstrating the success of a black individual at the forefront of an organisation or company was about more than personal accomplishment. It was about shattering stereotypes and proving that people of colour, including women, were just as capable.

For some, this might seem like an immense pressure or an over-emphasis on representation. But to me, it was deeply personal. I couldn't bear the thought of failing and subsequently causing setbacks for future generations. When people discuss role models and inspiration, my motivation was clear: I didn't want my actions to make things harder for the next person. This was my way of framing responsibility to myself. I've thought about it many times, especially in relation to my father, with whom I share my name. Every time I walked into a room, people's reactions were shaped by their perceptions of that name, and as I rose through the ranks in my career, it became even more challenging to shed that persona. What most people don't know is that 'Darcus' is a nickname that was given to my father by his bredrin back in Trinidad.

People can have certain expectations of you based on your reputation, and you feel the pressure to always be 'on' and maintain that image they've come to associate with you. But after a while, it becomes something you can't escape and any deviation from that expected demeanour becomes noticeable. What my father's death reminded me of is the generational nature of 'the struggle'. From the Royal African Company and three centuries of slave trading to the rise of the Black Lives Matter movement, black people in the West are on a constant daily grind for freedom, equality and respect. Some look at me and say, 'But Darcus, you made it. What's your problem?' In a way, this 'colour blindness' or liberal racism is as bad or worse than the in-your-face discrimination many black people experience every day because it implies that inequality is simply a state of mind, and an inability to pull up one's socks and get on with it. But look around. In Britain or Europe or even America, how many black CEOs of major corporations are there? As much as I love being an inspiration, I hate the exceptionalism that comes with it. Is it any wonder that so many young black men feel that success is beyond their reach in the corporate world or professions when there are so few of us at the top leading the charge?

For me, this is where leadership comes in. Anyone can say 'fuck the system' and take to the streets, Molotov cocktail in hand. But the ultimate act of rebellion is taking charge, having a sense of purpose and standing on that hill. Any fool can throw a brick through a window and call themselves a rebel. But in isolation, that changes nothing. Instead, we should strive to create a movement where people want to use those same bricks to build an equitable society as my father did and as I am trying to do in my own way.

10

You Can Get It If You Really Want

You can get it if you really want
But you must try, try and try, try and try
You'll succeed at last

— Desmond Dekker[1]

It's not every day of the week that an awkward and aloof 'kid' from the back streets of west London gets to sit in the studio with U2, one of the greatest rock 'n' roll bands of all time, but there I was, skinny lickle me, with the band's producer, Paul Epworth, inside a magnificently converted Victorian church in north London perched across a mixing desk from living legends Bono and The Edge. Having been in the room with the band on many occasions, and not being given to star-fucking, it was in many respects business as usual, but the fact that the album was a deeply personal body of work from the band, and had been delayed for some time, not least because Bono had recently

---

[1] Jimmy Cliff; Trojan Records.

undergone life-saving open-heart surgery, made the encounter all the more poignant.

A youthful-looking middle-aged technical whizz, Paul wasn't without his own stripes, having worked with the likes of Adele and Rihanna, and remixed tracks for a myriad of artists, from P. Diddy and Coldplay to New Order and Nine Inch Nails. As he pressed buttons, twiddled knobs and did whatever it is producers do, The Edge insisted I earn my corn as 'the boss' and listen to two mixes of the same track from *Songs of Experience* – the work at hand and U2's fourteenth studio album.

As one track after the other played, faded out and ended, I had no idea what I was meant to be listening to. To my ear, they both sounded *exactly* the same, i.e. very U2, very amazing. Sure, there was the subtlest of nuances between the two mixes, which The Edge's bionic-like hearing could differentiate from a mile away, but to my relatively untutored ear all I had was the faintest of opinions, which, given the company I was currently keeping, didn't mean shit.

'So, whaddya think?' The Edge said, leaning over to me, looking at me as though he were reaching into my soul for small change. Suddenly, Paul's eyes were on me too, as were Bono's, albeit behind a pair of Armani shades, which he wore less to be cool and more because of his glaucoma.

'Er . . . they're, er, great, great,' I said, giving it a faint shoulder shrug. 'Maybe, er, there was a bit more space in the, er, first mix? Er . . .'

Bono, The Edge and Paul looked at each other with a collective 'one more time, with feeling' and got back to work. I rocked back in my chair, clasped my hands and nodded to myself sagely. There are some acts in life that are impossible to feed back on, and there are others where your opinion matters more because, hey, they're not U2. When you're handling the biggest rock band on the planet, it's not your job to tell them to add a strings section or throw in a gospel choir on a track. My relationship with U2 was about giving them the resources they needed to do what they did best and making sure they felt totally loved and supported in their endeavours.

That said, I've always been a purist when it comes to how a record should sound. And while technology has indeed made it more accessible and faster for people to produce music, it's also led to some shortcuts. Studios used to be these grand spaces, but now everything you need can fit into a laptop. There's something magical about capturing the ambience of a room, miking up the instruments and having everyone play together. I totally get the appeal of programming and the convenience of digital, and I'm not against combining analogue with digital. Still, without the analogue touch, even if digital mimics some of those effects, you often lose that warmth and authenticity.

Even seasoned musicians get that technology can recreate some of these elements. But now, AI can compose a song and the results are astonishingly good. That said, technology has its place, and it's always been about evolving sounds. Think about it: when artists were producing in the '60s, they weren't aiming for a '50s vibe. They were aiming for something more forward-thinking. Like how *Sgt. Pepper's Lonely Hearts Club Band* pushed boundaries in terms of recording techniques. Everyone has always aimed for a futuristic sound, something distinct and fresh. U2 are no different..

After releasing the album *Songs of Innocence* in 2016, the band were back on Island, their 'spiritual home' following a seven-year separation. The split was due to Universal closing down Mercury, the band's long-time label, and then moving many of its acts to a new company, Virgin EMI. Bono, The Edge, Larry and Adam subsequently followed their closest ally at Island, former general manager Jason Iley, to Mercury, where he had jumped ship in 2005 to become MD.

Despite the tetchy parting of ways, U2 had kept Island's logo on its Mercury releases, as a mark of respect, which was a nice touch, and one that demonstrated the love the band had always had for us. When they took off, after twenty-six years at the label and international sales of over 150 million albums, they were our biggest act, and arguably the world's biggest band.

By the time they came back to Island, to a big fanfare, I was running the label by myself. It was like a homecoming; they were coming back to where they belonged. The afternoon they arrived, I got the whole office to down tools and gather on the shopfloor for a massive presentation with the band, which was followed by a standing ovation. Bono even sang in my ear, his mellifluous voice delivering a serenade I'll never forget. These guys are musical royalty. That was such a proud moment for me: a black man running the label that has the biggest rock band on the planet on its books. It was unheard of. The significance of U2's return was probably lost on most people in the office; but for me it was huge, not just because of the historical or cultural or even business significance, but because here were U2 looking at me now in a new light, looking at me as the guv'nor.

Back in the day, when I was a young up-and-coming A&R at Island, I had to choose my battles carefully. Most of the artists I handled were around my age, so my opinion didn't mean shit. But as I got older and more experienced, not only did my opinion hold more weight, but I also had an equal footing with major established artists, the successful artists on my roster who were ground-breaking, multi-platinum-selling, household names. Respecting their work but having the props to be respected in return meant that the conversations I had with the acts I repped were creative dialogues rather than me telling them what they should be doing.

Being in a room with U2, I was living the dream. Here I was, their guardian, their steward, the man marshalling the fortress around them, and, yes, as corny as it sounds, helping them be their best selves. What the hell did I know about arranging, engineering and mixing down an entire album? (That said, in truth, I think The Edge should've jacked up the bass a bit more on that track. As a black man, lemme tell ya, you can never have too much bass.)

Back in the day, I was just a young kid named Darcus trying to grind it out in the music industry. I'd proudly tell my friends and acquaintances, 'I work at Island Records, and Island Records is a big deal.' Back in '88, I was just thrilled to be part of it all and have the chance to turn a musical hobby into a musical career. But as success started rolling in with hits, promotions and pay rises, things changed. When David Joseph tapped me on the shoulder and said, 'Why don't you and Ted run the company?', my ambitions broadened, and I held my head a little higher. Then, when Ted left and I was flying solo, I was like, *Yeah, I've got this.*

However, having taken Island into the streaming era, collaborating with independent labels such as PMR and Communion, setting up the UK's first major label's black division, and after thirty years of being based in London, I'll admit, I had become a little jaded. So, when Universal Music UK's chairman and

CEO, and good friend, David Joseph called me into his office one morning in the spring of 2018 and asked, 'Darcus, do you want to run the American company?', suddenly ego, imposter syndrome and excitement all collided. It was one of those moments when your entire career flashes before your eyes. I was thinking, *Wow, they're asking me, so I must be good.* Still, doubt crept in. I'd always been part of a team, with talented people working under me, to my left, to my right and just above. I was like a creative midfielder, a playmaker – a Johan Cruyff, a Messi, a Zidane. Yes, I could score. I could make assists, create chances, deliver amazing passes. But could I lead *and* maintain my creative flair?

I never really saw myself as a leader and I don't think others did either. It was a surprise for sure. Fantastical football analogies aside, I'd always seen myself as more of an influencer than the top dog, albeit one without a massive Instagram or Twitter following. Regardless of network or audience size, influencing requires a certain set of skills that takes time to learn.

Throughout my career, I've always been conscious of the transient nature of people in this industry. I've witnessed talented people come and go, leaving their mark but eventually fading into memories or the stuff of dinner party anecdotes. Their names would occasionally crop up in discussions, but over time, they slowly became distant echoes, and then ghosts. Every now and again, especially during big A&R gatherings out at Theale Farm, you'd talk about these characters' accomplishments, asking each other, 'Do you remember so-and-so?' Then you'd have a chuckle and move on. One thing's for sure: I didn't want to wind up being someone's punchline.

Having seen this pattern repeat itself with executives, artists and assorted professionals, I've come to accept that everyone's time in the spotlight eventually comes to an end. It's a natural progression, and I never deluded myself into thinking I would be the exception. But seriously, what was my next move? I walked around asking myself, *Are you content being part of all this? Is there a sense of validation? Am I really making a mark here in the UK?*

Time to phone a friend, again.

'Look, something mad has happened,' I told my wife, Alison, over the phone. 'I've been offered the job in America. I'm coming home.'

Then I called Mum. She was proud but worried about the idea of losing her son. Despite having remarried years ago, I was still her only child, and here I was, her closest kin, presumably leaving the country. She was proud, but she didn't want me to go.

That evening, I gathered the family around the kitchen table to discuss what was, admittedly, a fait accompli by now. Ultimately, I was never going to say no and that decision was reinforced by the significant financial offer that Universal put on the table in front of me.

Darcey was far from excited, at first. She didn't want to go. She was preparing to start university and, having gotten into all the unis she'd applied to, was obviously focused on staying in the UK. Darcus Jr was the eager beaver of the bunch. 'Let's go Dad, let's go!' he said, revelling in the idea of all the goodies America had to offer. Alison had her initial reservations. How would she cope without her family and support network in London? Without her friends that she had known since school? It was going to be a big upheaval for the family, but despite her misgivings, she supported my decision all the way.

It's fair to say that the salary and relocation package helped to seal the deal. In return, all I had to do was run one of the most successful labels in the world, bag a bunch of number ones, sell a shit load of records and return consistent profits year on year. No pressure!

Yes, it was going to be a massive challenge, but how could I say no to such an offer? I asked myself: What does ambition look like? What have you worked for? What does success look like? And all roads led to this moment. Every time I walked into a school, a college or a university to give young people a pep talk, I always told them, 'Never miss out. Never miss the opportunity. Always seize the moment.'

While the family had their doubts, back at Island, David and Lucian were unequivocal in their support. 'Why don't you just go to America and meet with them, and let them sell it to you?' said David, bending my arm.

So, just a few days after learning about the position, I was on a plane to New York. I spent two days there, met with the Americans, returned, and then said, 'Cool, let's knock up a deal.'

Of course, I was familiar with everyone who was anyone in the Universal system, so I knew who I'd be talking to. There was Lucian, of course, Executive Vice President Michelle Anthony and CEO of Republic Records Monte Lipman. During that period of negotiations, I must have gone to New York about three or four times. I then went to LA to meet Lucian at Coachella festival in April to seal the deal, then off to Tobago with the family for a much-needed holiday before heading to New York, where I had now started to base myself.

The music industry likes to move quickly, never wants to be exposed, and always seeks to control the narrative, but I was still negotiating the package with the board. In America, outgoing Island US CEO David Massey was about to reveal his plans, so the board informed me they wanted to announce my move. While the negotiations were still ongoing, business had to continue as the final terms of the deal were agreed.

At Universal's annual conference, which was held at the Design Museum in Kensington, I was set to present our plans for the year to the company, which was odd, given the situation. Post-conference, rumours about my potential move to New York started spreading and colleagues from both the UK and the US began reaching out to me. Truth be told, I felt that things at Island UK had gotten stale for me, so now it wasn't so much a case of *if* I was going, but when. I didn't want to keep it a secret from those closest to me, even though the deal wasn't entirely finalised. People had started to speculate. I couldn't keep schtum any longer. It was time to address the rumours.

The next day, I gathered the bulk of the company in the boardroom, some forty-plus people. The news, from the horse's mouth, still took everyone by surprise, despite all the rumours. As soon as I made the announcement there was a palpable shift in the room, an easiness. It's almost comical to witness how quickly your influence wanes. You can feel your authority slipping away, as if it's physically leaving your fingertips. That sense of command you once held starts to vanish because people recognise the changing dynamic. They're aware that you're no longer the present nor the future of the situation. I observed people who seldom interacted before walking into each other's offices and engaging in hushed conversations. The atmosphere in the whole building changed.

Understandably, my team was worried about how this change might affect them and their individual roles within the company. People often start to contemplate their own future and wonder what the new leadership will mean for their positions, responsibilities and prospects. Minutes turned into hours, and days went by with people huddling together, engaging in discussions about the upcoming transition. They were speculating about who might be coming in to replace me and how it could impact the label's direction.

Here I was, an integral part of the organisation, someone synonymous with the company itself, jumping ship, albeit to resurface on another bigger, brasher part of the ship. I'd become a bit of a legend at Island. In fact, if Island was a football club, there would've been a massive mural of my face on the wall outside of it. (Okay, that sounds wank, but it's MY story and I'll lie if I want to.) I knew that some of the team were disappointed that I was leaving, but I was convinced that it was time for a new chapter. It was essential to embrace change, move forward, feel the fear and do it anyway.

Well, that's what I kidded myself into believing.

I remember talking to my boss right before I was due to take a few weeks of holiday. 'I might as well take my holiday and not come back,' I told him. It seemed like the best choice for me, instead of sitting there with everyone knowing I wasn't part of the future. 'It's not a productive use of my time, and it would just waste yours. It's better for you to start the succession planning, and for me to prepare for what's next.'

It would allow the staff to prepare for the changes ahead. The certainty they once had under my leadership was now giving way to uncertainty and a feeling of apprehension, as there were mixed feelings about where their loyalties should now lie and whether it was even worth investing any time in me. I'd soon be gone, after all, and they'd have another boss to cosy up to.

Spring had sprung and the announcement came that, as of 1 July 2018, I would become the new president of Island Records

US – the first black Briton to become the head of a major US record label. It was the achievement of a lifetime. From here, there was only really one more rung I could climb on the corporate ladder, and that was to become the head of an entire entertainment multinational, namely Universal Music Group, which had a market cap of $50 billion. Not bad for a kid who left school at sixteen with no qualifications and most likely undiagnosed ADHD.

Of course, the first thing on the corporate agenda was to make a public announcement, namely draft a suitably upbeat press release, which was a very American thing to do. When the champagne starts popping and the flashbulbs start going off, everyone and their aunt wants to take the credit and puff themselves up.

On paper, and publicly, the decision for me to go out to the US was spectacular. Everyone was thrilled with the idea. When they pitched it to me, they explained how the board had been unanimously excited. They all believed it was a fantastic idea and celebrated with high-fives. As I reflected on my experiences – my achievements, my bits, my interactions with notable figures and institutions like the Palace, Amy Winehouse and Island Records – the entire narrative *did* seem outstanding. The press release that was sent out looked so impressive that I even thought of toning down some parts. Not everything mentioned was solely my achievement; others had played roles too, and, unlike many in the industry, I felt embarrassed and guilty about taking credit for other people's hard work.

Nevertheless, when I first read the news in the trade press announcing my move to America, I was in awe. The person they described seemed remarkable! *Who the hell is* this *superstar?* I thought. The story painted me as incredibly successful and competent, but I wondered how others would perceive it. Some might be thinking, *Let's see how he fares in America* . . . It was a mix of emotions – a combination of confidence and apprehension.

In some ways, stepping up to become the CEO of a major label was a bit like being a driving instructor in a car with dual controls. On the one hand, you're moving forwards, driving things through; on the other hand, you're constantly reflecting, monitoring and evaluating what you, or, more critically, those in the hot seat, are doing. This is the yin and yang of leadership. It's not always about asserting your opinion, but rather supporting and elevating the passions of others. It's about being inspired by their enthusiasm, regardless of whether you fully comprehend their vision. Leadership isn't about dominating the wheel but knowing when to take control to prevent mishaps, and when to let go. Ego can sometimes obstruct this balance, making us forget to trust and back others. Reflecting means being supportive of their unique tastes and ideas because that's where innovation thrives. Recognise your strengths and play to them.

Look, I'm a fifty-something guy, so my perspective is that of a fifty-something guy – albeit a pretty cool one. The ideas I had as a 24-year-old and the cultural context I inhabit in my fifties are totally different. Whenever I begin working with an artist, audience or market, my initial approach is to ask, 'What about you?', instead of dictating, 'You should do this.' I'm not here to dictate terms. My role is to guide and hope that individuals can rise to the occasion.

The role of a leader is to create guardrails, ensuring the path is clear for success. It's not about restricting people's paths but ensuring they have a direction and a boundary within which they can explore, innovate and sometimes even fuck up. I've always believed you should allow people to fuck up – you should almost *make* them fuck up. Yes, it's a cliché, but that's where you learn the most. Anyone who wants to have a career in the music business is probably going to make a lot of mistakes, so if you know that, then you won't be frightened of things going pear-shaped. And all you've got to do is have the steel and determination to rectify or move on. In America, however, it felt like there was no margin for error. It was a case of one strike and you're out. All of which meant that even thinking of failure wasn't an option.

I've always said, my job involves making a ton of decisions, signing off on countless things over the years – millions and millions of pounds involved. I mean, I'd have to be terrible not to get a *single* thing right; so, when people start bragging about how amazing they are, it makes me a bit cautious. Actions speak louder. That's why I've always thought that the craft of what we do is so important. Being able to say, 'I was there in the studio when these records were being made,' as opposed to just signing off on something and putting it out there. It's all about the truth of being a real A&R person. At least that's how I see it.

With the exception of a couple of 'trial separations', when I got the offer from Island US, I'd been at the label for thirty years. This wasn't just a job. It was a career; a life's work. My relationship with Island had lasted longer than most people's marriages. I was in that rarefied club of global leaders who had started out in the mailroom, as an intern, or, as some people liked to say condescendingly, as 'the tea boy', to become their company's CEO.

I'd never been one to take the easy route or the quick handout, and having started from the bottom, I could puff my chest out and say I stood for something. I was a grafter, and I'd got to where I'd got to on merit, not because my dad played golf with someone else's dad, or they were at Eton or Cambridge together. When I started out in 1988 as an office assistant, I was just over the moon that I'd got a job in the music industry – at Island Records no less. Then, after the six-month trial, I was just happy that I'd got the job full-time. I was on something like six-and-a-half grand a year. Then it went to £10K, and then, I was just happy to be around. Then I became a scout, and it became about who I'd love to sign . . .

'Few in the music industry have Darcus's track record of creative and commercial success,' Lucian told anyone who'd listen. 'I've had the pleasure over the years of working closely with Darcus, who has impeccable creative instincts and takes a long-term view of artist development. I'm thrilled he is taking on this new role and I'm excited to support him in signing, developing and breaking many more artists.'

I genuinely cared about what I was doing. I wasn't a career politician. My mum always emphasised the difference between politicians who enter the field for the right reasons, often coming from a background of activism and bringing their protest-driven mindset into politics, and those with ambitions of becoming Prime Minister or just advancing their careers. I didn't follow a traditional path, such as going to art school or studying sociology at university and then ending up in the music industry. My journey has always been driven by my passion and commitment to what I believe in, 100 per cent.

Before I accepted the US gig, I ran into my old friend, mentor, guiding light and moral compass, Chris Blackwell, at a U2 gig at Madison Square Garden in New York, which was part of their two-leg, sixty-concert, Experience + Innocence tour. Backstage, everyone was buzzing; sweat was practically dripping off the walls. I gave Adam Clayton a big hug, told him what an amazing show it had been, and then Chris took me by the arm and leant in, his voice barely audible over the hullabaloo.

'Good luck in America, Darcus. You know it's going to be bloody hard over there, don't you?' he cautioned.

'No shit,' I said with a sarcastic grin.

Later, Bono wrote me a lovely letter, a lyrical pat on the back, or an *attaboy* as they say in the States, in which he wished me the best and hoped I'd take a 'big slice out of the Apple' now that I'd finally become CEO of one of the most iconic record labels in the world.

While I might not have some specific technical skills, like being able to make a chest of drawers or produce a record for that matter, I had been entrusted with millions and millions of pounds over the years to make critical decisions on signing artists and investing in them and their work. I'd officially made it. I was now the caporegime of Island Records.

Nevertheless, not for the first time in my life, I was about to overestimate my spirit, and underestimate just how Babylonian the music business could really be.

11

Empire State of Mind

Yeah, I'm out that Brooklyn, now I'm down in Tribeca
Right next to De Niro, but I'll be hood forever
I'm the new Sinatra, and since I made it here
I can make it anywhere, yeah, they love me everywhere

— Jay-Z[1]

I'd been going back and forth to America since the late '80s, but no matter how much you think you have the measure of the Big Apple, it's not until you live and work there that you really 'get it'. Running Island UK was one thing. Running Island US was a whole new proposition. This was America. I was inheriting a completely different roster from the one I had helped to build in the UK over the course of three decades. It was a totally different model. And I was working with Americans, all over the US: black America, white America, Hispanic

---

[1] Shawn Carter, Alexander Shuckburgh, Janet Sewell-Ulepic, Angela Hunte, Alicia Keys, Sylvia Robinson, Bert Keyes; Roc Nation.

America, which was a new one for me. New York work culture was something else. They're animals – brutal. To a New Yorker, taking a two-week holiday is like a sabbatical. That's why there are coffee shops and vitamin stores and clinics and drug dealers on every street corner in New York. Because everyone is maxed out or running on empty, they need caffeine or guarana or taurine or something a little stronger to keep going. They're hardcore, man.

Moving from a world I knew like the back of my hand to a semi-strange new one in New York was an eye-opening experience, which, given the physical, visual, sonic, emotional and spiritual dynamics of the Big Apple, was a full-on D-Day assault on the senses.

For starters, I'd gone from Island UK's cosy boho three-storey offices in west London to Universal Music Group's stunning skyscraper HQ at 1755 Broadway in midtown Manhattan, right in the heart of the city's theatre district. Just walking into the joint was a trip.

UMG was no joke. It is the leading record label in the world, boasting an impressive roster of sub-labels and artists from more than sixty countries. According to the company's most recent financial statements, recorded music remains UMG's most lucrative business segment, generating higher revenue streams than music publishing and merchandising combined. Universal was the label with the highest share in the recorded music market worldwide in 2020, accounting for roughly 32 per cent of combined physical and digital music trade revenue that year. Meanwhile, revenue generated from Universal Music Group's music publishing segment surpassed $1 billion for the third year in a row, reaching $1.34 billion globally.

Aside from finding out who ground the best coffee beans and who sold the best cinnamon and raisin bagels in the neighbourhood, one of my first tasks was introducing myself to my new sister company.

As I'd helped break several US artists in the UK, including Ariana Grande, DNCE, Drake, Hailee Steinfeld, Nick Jonas, Nicki M, Post Malone and The Weeknd, I was at least *something* of a known quantity stateside. But here I was, fresh off the plane, having landed this killer job with a seven-figure package, while others in the New York office had been in their roles in America for years, and I just breezed into town and took their food. No one made me feel out of place or anything, but you'd have to be naïve not to think some might have had thoughts about it.

I walked into Island's plush, expansive boardroom flanked by the head of HR and the head of PR. It was like something out of *Mad Men*. As the plate-glass doors swung open, I was confronted by some forty-odd mostly bright-eyed and bushy-tailed faces, all of them trying to get a read of me. I took to the stage area of the office, with a big, warm smile, trying to make a good first impression. As I addressed the team, I sensed various reactions from the audience. Some appeared cool and composed, others seemed eager to be impressed, while a few seemed somewhat uncertain. It wasn't a tough crowd, but it was no kids' birthday party, either.

As I stood there, an English voice in a room full of New Yorkers, I couldn't help but feel a mix of excitement and nervousness. Being British, I decided to rely on my charm and wit to win them over – you know, razzle dazzle 'em with a touch of the Hugh Grants.

Standing there in that boardroom, cracking carefully vetted jokes, name dropping and namechecking felt like a performance. I wanted to convey confidence and authority while being approachable and genuine. It was a challenging balancing act, given that I just wanted to get the fuck out of there, get back to my office and admire the Manhattan skyline as I figured out what the hell I was going to do for the next few years.

During those first weeks, no one explicitly made me uncomfortable, but I couldn't shake the feeling that conversations about me were happening behind closed doors, in those gossipy little groups by the Nespresso machine or the watercooler. Why? Because that's what happens in all organisations whenever there's change. You didn't need to be Lee Iacocca to figure that one out. I hadn't grown up with these people, and I hadn't worked at another company other than Universal for decades, so for the first time in a long time, I felt like a complete outsider. My knowledge of the workplace was limited to the Universal system, and now I had to learn an entirely new corporate language in an unfamiliar landscape. Often, I found myself having to downplay or suppress certain aspects of my character to fit in or adapt to a specific social context to be 'woke'. The US was way hipper to relational sensitives and interactions than the UK, where you could, in the right environment, get away with being a bit of a dickhead without getting served. In the US, if your face didn't fit, you could wind up looking at a multimillion-dollar lawsuit just for leaving the toilet seat up.

Stepping into this new position and environment was certainly a tough ground to navigate, but I took it as an opportunity to learn, grow and adapt. I knew that establishing a strong connection with the team and building trust would be crucial for the organisation's success. Luckily, I came with a bit of track record. But then people say, 'So, you're in our town now, prove it again!' I think my resume got me through the door. Even if it was a bit shaky meeting the team at first, the company knew that my CV was sound.

Intriguingly, after I'd addressed the troops, many of the black employees approached me on the side, expressing their pride and support for me. It was heart-warming to get a vote of confidence from the brothas and sistas, because just as African-American actors liked to gripe about black British actors 'coming over 'ere and stealing all our Oscar-winning roles', the same could be said of the music industry due to the racial – and racist – dynamics of the industry.

It took me a while to appreciate that 'Blackness' in America was very different to that in the UK. The African-American community rolls differently over there, not least because, on the one hand, it's more homogenous than Britain's black community, which numbers just under 2.5 million and is roughly split down the middle between those of Afro-Caribbean and those of African descent. Throw in another 1 million people of mixed heritage and you have an Afrocentric 'of colour' population that's cleaved from three very distinct backgrounds. It also only makes up 3 per cent of the UK population compared with the near-on 13 per cent of America's 332 million who are black, but largely African-American. Because of this difference in scale, and history, namely a black immigrant UK population versus a black US population with a direct, in-situ link to a past mired in the horrors of slavery, there is a much bigger black middle class in the US compared with the UK. Consequently, Atlanta's black community, say, is markedly different to New York's, and within New York, Brooklyn's community is different to Queens, and so on. Sure, there's a difference in second-generation Caribbeans from London and those from, say, Leeds, but it's largely superficial.

When I arrived at Island US, there were only two other black executives in similar positions: Jon Platt, who went from being CEO of Warner Chappell Music to chairman and CEO of Sony/ATV Music Publishing while I was based in New York; and Sylvia Rhone, who became chairwoman and CEO of Epic Records in 2019. I was now the new kid on the block, a black Englishman in New York, not just overseeing an urban music roster or performing as a tap-dancing VP or senior VP but running the show as a CEO. As remarkable as that felt, I couldn't escape the fact that the position was culturally and historically loaded.

As with the sports entertainment industry, a large swathe of the US music industry's talent pool is African-American, but the lack of diversity at the top level was shocking. In the States, gender, more than race, was the issue that was tapping away at the glass ceiling, so being a black British male meant that no doubt I was viewed with suspicion because I was such an outlier.

Maybe one of the added problems I had with the American corporate culture was people mistaking my 'coolness' for indifference. Often, the doubters, the critics, the detractors and the haters only see the edited highlights of someone with a public persona. In interviews, for instance, I'd often feel like the interviewer was chasing me for information because of my self-deprecating nature. Because I don't come across as bragging or trying to be the centre of attention, I present as being quite different from a lot of Americans, which, as you see with pop stars and politicians and public figures alike, is all 'me, me, me'.

The road to success might look the same for some, but for many of us, it's a unique and often more challenging journey because of the pressure to 'represent' the community as well as satisfy the needs of artists, fans, bosses and shareholders.

For my first three or four months in New York, from April to July, I lived in a suite at the W Hotel on Times Square, right in the heart of Manhattan, just a couple of blocks from Universal. For the first couple of weeks, I loved it, but the novelty soon wore off – I needed my own space.

On 5 July, I moved into a twelfth-floor apartment right by Central Park. Alison had been travelling back and forth since I moved to New York, looking into schools for Darcus Jr, but she was still packing up our shit in London, putting things in storage and generally taking care of business. I'd now been in New York on my own for four months. It was mad and bizarre and pretty discombobulating, if I'm honest.

I'd get up in the morning, open the blinds and look out at the New York skyline, then look down onto the street and be like, *Shit, that's Broadway down there.* I'd leave the apartment, walk or jog or scoot down Broadway, and bowl into work thinking, *Man, I live out here.* And it's lovely, and it's exciting, and you get into the office and you're working with these people; Americans in an American workspace with American culture, with real New Yorkers. Yet, living on the Upper West Side, on my block, there weren't many people like me around, certainly not ones who weren't delivering something or sweeping something up.

By August 2018, Alison, Darcus and Darcey had joined me in New York. We all had to shift gears to keep up with Manhattan's relentless pace; it was a whole new ballgame compared with London, or even other American cities I was familiar with, like

Boston or San Francisco. My calendar was jam-packed and the city's buzz kept me constantly on my toes. But NYC wasn't just about the hustle; it was also about immersing myself in its rich musical and cultural tapestry. Many evenings found me out in Brooklyn, hopping from one live music venue to another, stumbling upon fresh talent and enjoying shows. Sure, the commute between NYC and Brooklyn took a chunk of time, but it was all part and parcel of living in such a dynamic city.

One evening, I was out with Lucian Grainge at some big songwriting Hall of Fame shindig in the city. It was one of the first major events I'd attended since moving to America and Lucian was being honoured with the Howie Richmond Hitmaker Award. There I was rubbing shoulders and pressing flesh with the likes of Neil Diamond, Usher and Mariah Carey when I ran into Abel Tesfaye, aka The Weeknd.

'So, Darcus. You're out here now?' asked Abel.

'Yeah, you know, I'm just gonna see how it goes,' I said, playing it cool, semi-scanning the room, checking out the competition's sneaker game. You can tell a lot about a person from their sneakers, BTW. Anyway, Lucian overheard our conversation and cut me a look like Mum would give me when I got a detention.

'Never tell anyone, "We'll see how it goes," because you'll never win a deal,' said Lucian, eyeballing me. 'If people start thinking that you're only here for a holiday and then you're buggering off home, they won't invest in you.'

I was being schooled on a basic point, but the sort of casual remark I could get away with in the UK wouldn't cut it in the US. The stakes were just way, *way* bigger now. Literally, some bullshit could come tumbling out of my mouth and Universal's share price would crash.

'This is your home, Darcus,' Lucian added. 'Don't forget that.'

From that point on, whenever I had to head back to London, I'd say, 'I'm going to London,' not 'I'm going home.' And when I was in London, or wherever, and I was going back to New York, I'd say, 'I'm going home.' Such semantics were crucial to my new profile, and the wider brand values and economic reality I was representing. I had enough swag to change tack and convince business associates, shareholders, the press and the odd $300-million pop star that the Big Apple was now home. The only person I was yet to convince, however, was myself.

Despite the occasional mishap, the music industry allowed me to get up close and personal with some of my musical heroes. Generally, I don't allow myself to be overawed by celebrity or let fandom get in the way of professionalism, because that's not cool, unless it is Chuck D, of course. Or the Specials, who I once hustled into taking a fanboy with me. These acts weren't the biggest pop stars of all time, but they helped shape my view of the world.

As the honeymoon period started to fade away, the weight of responsibility I'd taken on really hit me. I was no longer the familiar figure I once was in the UK, and I didn't have the family and friendship networks close to hand to call on if I needed advice over brunch or a few laughs with some old buddies over a joint. I started to question myself: did I even want to be here? Is money everything? Maybe it's not? But then the money started rolling in, and the economics shifted. Years of being mulched up in the corporate meat grinder had taught me how to bite my tongue, take the money and run, because, well, the money is good. Everyone wants to come off like a maverick, but as Mike Tyson famously said, 'Everyone has a plan until [they're] punched in the mouth.' It's the same with money. Everyone is Karl Marx until they get that big fat cheque. It's then when you ask yourself, 'Am I just in it for the dough now? Have I sold out? How do I find my way back to my true self?'

People would ask me all the time about my accent. 'So, where are you from?' or, 'I love your accent' every time I opened my mouth in public. I was the proverbial Englishman in New York. Because I travelled frequently around the States, I was used to the 'accent thing', which of course was doubly amplified by being both black and British. I could wind up in a gas station in Nowheresville, filling up and getting some cigarettes, and instantly it'd be, 'OMG! What's that accent? Are you English? Australian? I *love your accent!*' It never got irritating. In fact, I think for some people, it took the edge off some potentially awkward situations. It also helped to galvanise 'brand Darcus' to an extent.

Day in, day out, I'd arrive at the office in what I call 'foreman's mode'. I'd have to be up for it, constantly. You've got to be a leader, keep everyone on their toes, win deals, handle HR, show empathy, all while being the figurehead the team looks up to, and the board wants out there representing. Then, just like that, I'd leave the office, and walk, jog or scoot the couple of blocks back home, back to my regular self, dealing with the road rage of the day and just wanting to flop on the sofa, watch TV and crash out. Then, the following morning, it would start all over again. It was like living in that old Disney skit with Goofy, where he goes from being a happy family guy to a devilish road-rage nutter as soon as he gets in his car and heads to work.

For the first time in my life, I didn't so much feel like I was suffering from imposter syndrome, as this 'condition' presupposes that you're you, but just bullshitting your way through a job or a role you don't feel qualified to do. No, now I felt like I was properly leading a double life. People had a perception of me at work, which I couldn't really blame them for having, but it was a perception based on an act. Having to do that ten, twelve, sixteen hours a day was not only exhausting, but it left me questioning myself, existentially. I mean, who am I really? Was the act an extension of me, a protective shield I put up, an alter ego, or some other guy that inhabited my subconsciousness? Worse yet, was the act the real me, and the me I *thought* was me a phoney me?

Man, I needed help.

12

Move On Up

Take nothing less
Than the supreme best
Do not obey rumours people say
'Cause you can pass the test

– Curtis Mayfield[1]

In the American business landscape, the 'C suite' refers to the executive level, including CEOs, CFOs, COOs, etc. These top-level executives are often associated with privileges and perks, such as having a driver at your beck and call, your own parking space, first-class travel, luxurious accommodation, expense accounts and so forth.

Back in the UK, being the president was markedly different from being a CEO in America. In the UK, I wasn't the CEO; that was David Joseph's role, and he had a very different way of operating. I probably adapted my style in the US to match

---

[1] Curtis Mayfield; Curtom Records.

his. So, even though I held the title of president of the company, I was effectively the president *and* CEO.

This distinction, or lack thereof on my part, caused something of an uproar in the black community during a period in which the Black Lives Matter movement had become very vocal about the under-representation of, and credit for, black people in the corporate realm.

One day, I received a call from Universal's communications team, telling me about online chatter from a figure in the American music industry called Chris Anokute. Chris had been making noise and complained to anyone who'd listen that I didn't have the title of CEO even though I was now running the company. A former senior vice-president of A&R at the Island Def Jam Music Group, Chris was an executive producer on *American Idol* and ran his own entertainment company, Young Forever Inc., so his opinion mattered, at least on a corporate level. I was taken aback because I knew I was the CEO. However, the issue arose because the CEO title was omitted from my press release when I moved to America, something I hadn't noticed at the time.

This oversight caused quite a stir, especially with some people in the black community who had genuine concerns about the lack of CEO recognition. It was a source of tension. I even had to contact Anokute to clarify the situation, assuring him that I was indeed the CEO, and that the omission was unintentional. Eventually, they had to amend my Wikipedia page to correctly reflect my position as CEO, but the whole situation had caused unnecessary controversy. In some ways it was an illustration of British insouciance versus American attention to detail. In a country without gongs and peerages but chockful of insecurity,

credits and titles matter. That's why Americans love philan-
thropy. You know, there's nothing better for a rich American
than to have their name on a big gold plaque over the entrance
to a library or a sports arena.

For me, representation, facilitation, and now leadership at the
very top, was about purpose, not profit. I was in the business
of making money to make music, not making music to make
money. But whether you're a writer, an actor, a director, a
painter, a singer or a band, breaking America is the Holy Grail.
Many British acts have tried, and failed, from Cliff Richard to
the Kinks to Oasis. For me, crossing the Atlantic and supping
from that sacred cup meant working with the top songwriters
and producers who make great-sounding records – records that
sound better than whatever it was we were making in our own
backyard. But I had to work my way into these cats' studios,
and that meant making hits not just in the UK but in the US,
too. Having transatlantic successes gets you in a room with that
calibre of songwriting and production talent.

As the new head of a major international label, coming out of
the traps, what I didn't need were one-hit wonders, novelty acts,
half-baked bands or mutton dressed as lamb. That's not to say
that all I wanted to sign or deal with were no-brainers or guarantee hit-makers, because in the music industry every deal comes
with an element of huge risk – because you're investing so much
time, energy and financial resources to make an artist successful. But like the incoming president of a nation, as an incoming
CEO, like it or not, often you're saddled with the legacy or poor
mistakes of the previous administration.

When I got to America, for instance, Skip Marley, Bob's
grandson, had signed to Island a few years earlier. He was in

the throes of making an album, and had been working with some talented people, but they were from Sweden. Now, I've got nothing at all against Sweden, but Swedes making a reggae album, with Bob Marley's grandson? Ha! I guess you could call it a concept album! If you are from the Caribbean, or have anything to do with the Caribbean, you would listen to it and think, *Nah, nah. That sounds* wrong. So, I scrapped all the songs. It cost a lot of dough, but the way I explained my decision was thus: One, a Marley should not be making this kind of record. Two, Bob wouldn't like it. Three, without Bob Marley, there would be no Island Records. His album *Legend* never left the charts, so Skip gets a pass. That's how important an artist's back catalogue is. The music business isn't just about signing acts, getting them in the studio and recording new material. Often, it's about managing back catalogues. Catalogue is as important as, if not more important than, signing new acts, because it's the catalogue side of a label's business that allows it to go and invest in new talent.

So, when it comes down to what my offering is as a label CEO, it's about doing the right bits of business; sometimes that means having to junk someone like Skip Marley's material, sometimes that means reissuing some old-school hip-hop on a limited-edition release. The history of the music industry in the United States also reflects how corporate decisions and power dynamics can influence the trajectory of black music, labels and artists. The assimilation of black labels by larger corporate entities and the rebranding of black artists as pop acts can lead to an erasure of their cultural uniqueness. Rebalancing the power structure in the music industry, and the corporate space, period, through greater diversity and representation isn't just about putting more boots on the ground. You only have to look at how colonialism worked, or how some Western regimes or corporations use tokenism to know that putting a bunch of black or brown yes men in overseeing positions changes nothing. Whether it's a government using black ministers to sell racist immigration policy to a largely white electorate or unconscious bias leading to culturally dubious branding, marketing or, yes, music, authentic diversity and representation isn't simply about numbers or optics: it's about doing the right thing. Doing the right thing means not waiting until the twenty-first century to remove golliwogs from jam jars, drop the name 'Redskins' from your NFL franchise, or make reggae music that sounds like it came out of an accordion at the Munich Oktoberfest.

The music business is littered with the bodies of pop stars (and A&Rs) who traded on a family name, were in a band but then went solo, or made the mistake of thinking a hit in one market would guarantee world domination. Remember Michelle Williams? Exactly. She was the first member of Destiny's Child to go solo, and while she had some success in the US gospel charts, she never set the world on fire in the pop or R&B charts. Another Williams who flopped was Robbie, but not as a solo act. Patently, when he left Take That, he continued to smash it as a solo artist. Just not in America. They didn't get him over there; he was too provincial or maybe even ironic. Recognising those records with the potential to transcend borders is a skill that comes with experience. When you're involved with such records, you can't help but think, *This is going to go around the world.* These are the records that change the game. Experiencing that kind of success once makes you hungry for it again. You understand where the bar is set, and you strive to meet and exceed it.

Over the years, I've seen the industry standards shift from a low bar to something much higher, mainly because the audience or the market is more discerning these days. Greater choice, and greater access to information, has meant that musical tastes have become more eclectic. People want the best there is to offer across genres rather than settle for, say, yet another guitar band, because labels are in a guitar band cycle and thus shoving that down people's throats. That won't wash in a multichannel, multimedia, social-media environment. Much of this bar-raising, and higher expectation or quality control also comes down to the rise of mash-up culture. It's no coincidence that coming from a diverse background, and having a multicultural family, has a major influence over my musical tastes and curatorial eye. It's fascinating to observe the shifting cultural landscape, especially when it comes to music and the acceptance of artists from diverse backgrounds. Today, we see young white artists who have grown up in neighbourhoods with a significant black influence, and they are fully embraced by audiences. Artists like Devlin, OR and many white rappers are receiving recognition and respect for their talents, rather than being stigmatised as Vanilla Ice was in the past for being a 'wigger'.

These young artists have grown up in environments where they've been exposed to the realities of life in the hood and have absorbed elements of gang culture. Whether they're in predominantly white areas or not, they've blended these experiences with patois and street culture, and it resonates with a wide audience. It's like they've authentically integrated these influences into their music and identities.

This kind of assimilation might not be as evident in the United States, but it does happen, especially when artists are embraced by their communities for their genuine connection to the culture. Artists like Bubba Sparxxx from the South brought a unique country rap style to the forefront. Compared to the past, when the likes of Marky Mark faced criticism for cultural appropriation, it's remarkable to see how much more inclusive and accepting the music industry and its audiences have become. It reflects the evolving and diverse nature of music in contemporary society.

Take Elvis, for instance. He was an undeniably iconic figure who transcended boundaries. I used to listen to his music and watch his movies on a Saturday or during the summer holidays, likewise John Wayne (well, except for the music). Even Mum was an Elvis fan, but when Public Enemy's 'Fight the Power' came out in 1989, Chuck D threw a spanner in my works. Chuck raps, 'Elvis was a hero to most / But he never meant shit to me / Straight up racist that sucker was / Simple and plain,' before Flavor Flav interjects, 'Motherfuck him and John Wayne.' I was like, *Dang!* Years later, Chuck clarified what many had taken to have originally been an all-out assault on Elvis for being a racist, but the truth of the lyric is far more subtle. Like many white artists in the music business, Elvis benefitted from white privilege and an overarching system of white supremacy without actively being a racist himself. If you're white, all you have to do is follow the rules and you get paid in full. If you're black, however, these rules don't apply.

Over time, people have become more open-minded in their approach to culture. There's a significant amount of overlap and blending in the Venn diagram of cultures, and the lines between them have blurred. It's not so much about strict boundaries anymore.

Cultures have evolved into subcultures, and within those subcultures, you can find even more nuances and diversity. Language is no longer a barrier, as seen with the global success of acts like BTS and various Korean and Latin American records crossing over to international audiences.

Today, everything is less tribal, and there's a rich tapestry of mixing, hybridisation and diversity. Subcultures within subcultures have emerged, creating an intricate web of cultural expressions. Whether it's different strands of hip-hop, rock, or entirely new genres like math rock or emo rap, there's something for everyone to explore, and the possibilities are endless.

I believe that people are much more curious nowadays, and they possess the ability to satiate their curiosity, whether it's done rightly or wrongly. This curiosity has become evident in the way society is evolving. People seem to be striving to form their own opinions, independent of the narratives they are exposed to, whether those narratives are accurate or not.

Over the past decade, it has felt like the ground beneath us is constantly moving, like tectonic plates. We think we've found our footing, but then everything shifts again. Unlike before, when change occurred in cycles over the years, now it seems to happen on a daily basis.

I was six months into being the CEO of one of the world's most iconic record labels. Big office. Big desk. Big expectations. Most of the time I didn't want to think about it; I didn't want to listen to what anyone was saying about the position, the title, the fucking name badge. But that was easy for me to say. In America, the music business isn't just a $15 billion per annum industry; it's the nexus between the wider entertainment industry, professional sports, media, politics and technology. This is

The iconic Annie Lennox.

Hanging with Abel from the Weeknd.

Ladies and gentleman, Ms Mary J. Blige.

Drake, the early years.

Working with the legend
that is Cat Stevens.

My favourite Child,
don't @ me.

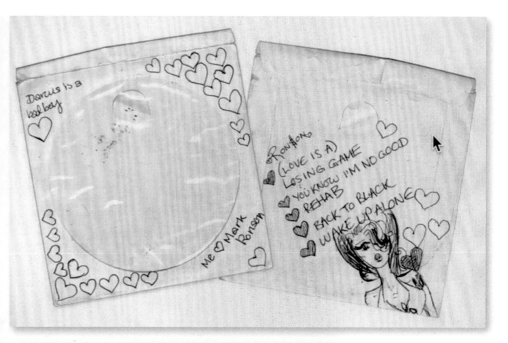

Above: Amy doodles 'Darcus is a bad boy' on the original Mark Ronson demos.

Left: BRITs night, 2005.

Right: Amy's squad.

Below: Twenty years later, the return match of Island Records versus the Marleys, 2007.

Presentation with Jessie J after selling out Shepherd's Bush Empire for the first time.

Rick Rubin, David Foster and John Janick at a Universal conference.

Disc presentation with Florence at the Kensington Hilton.

Above left: Signing KSI in his Prime.

Above right: When meeting one of your heroes doesn't disappoint.

Below: The Specials. Bucket list fulfilled, releasing their first album in forty years in the US. RIP Terry Hall.

Berry Gordy and
that is all.

Sean Mendes at the
Grammys: great artist,
great human being.

Right: Bossman Chris Blackwell.

Below: Someone forgot to order the 'L'.

why when an A-lister like Kanye West sneezes, America catches a cold. But this also breeds a level of arrogance that at times can be a touch, well, delusional.

An illustration of this point is when I flew out to meet Eddie Murphy at his home in Sacramento, California. I'd travelled to the other side of the States, nearly 3,000 miles, with the sole intention of pitching to Eddie for the soundtrack to his forth-coming movie, *Coming 2 America*, the sequel to *Coming to America*, undoubtedly one of his best films. When I got to his palatial 12,600-square-foot mansion, which would soon go on the market for a cool $10 million, I was ushered into his recording studio, where he was working on a new album, which he set about pitching to me as a sort of quid pro quo for the soundtrack deal.

As I sat down, Eddie produced an ornate wooden cigarette box and opened it to reveal several perfectly pre-rolled joints.

'You want one?' he said.

'Thanks, but no thanks. I'm trying to cut down,' I said, thinking to myself, *Eddie Murphy just offered me a joint. What the fuck?*

Soon, slightly 'off' reggae beats and cannabis smoke filled the air. Now, don't get me wrong, Eddie has a great voice, and some of the stuff he produced with Snoop Lion, aka Snoop Doggy Dogg, was, er, original if nothing else. But for me, coming from a British Caribbean background, as the head of Island Records – Bob Marley's label? Nah, man. Eddie's vibe just wasn't working for me.

After a lot of doo-dahing, tapping and humming, I start to think that there's no way I can get through this straight. So . . .

'Eddie, I think I will take you up on one of those joints after all . . .'

'Irie.'

Within minutes, I was stoned as fuck. The music sounded better, as everything does when you're stoned, but not better enough for me to sign on the dotted line.

'So, whaddya think?' said Eddie through the marijuana mist.

It's moments like these where you earn the big bucks.

'Interesting,' I said, working the English diplomat move.

It's also moments like these, certainly in the States, where having an English accent can clear a path to the exit.

'Yeah, it's really interesting, Eddie. Lemme talk it over with the team and get back to you.'

Suffice it to say, I didn't sign Eddie and I didn't get the movie soundtrack.

Incredibly, for a country that has a rich comedic tradition going back to Buster Keaton and Harold Lloyd, through to Richard Pryor and Eddie Murphy to Chris Rock and Dave Chappelle, there's a distinct lack of humour in the American workplace. Office banter just doesn't exist in the US. And you can't use the C-word for sure. People just lose their shit. I remember being in the boardroom one morning, early into my tenure as CEO. A few of us were sat around the table discussing an issue with the manager of one of our artists.

'Well, they can suck my dick,' I said with a faint chuckle.

Cue stunned silence, jaws dropping, ashen faces, maybe the odd 'whoa' under the breath.

After the meeting, the head of HR pulled me to one side. 'Hey, Darcus. How are you?'

'I'm fine.'

'How's your day?'

'Just grand.'

'Awesome. Just a quiet word . . . Back there . . . You can't say stuff like that.'

What might be considered a light-hearted joke in the UK can be seen as offensive or inappropriate in an American context. Americans tend to be more sensitive about certain topics, and there are stricter rules and guidelines in corporate settings to avoid any potential HR issues. That same HR woman wound up having a few more 'quiet words' with me over time. Sometimes I'd just make a throwaway comment and people would look at me with that 'whoa' expression as if I'd gone full David Brent.

When I moved over to Island US, I was actually given a handbook about transitioning to my new and different work culture, which explained the nuances of working with Americans, their approach to deals, their general work attitude, and other pseudo-organisational theories. I just kind of skim-read it, but the nub of it was: going to work in America was just like going to work in Japan: you had to adapt or risk offending a lot of colleagues.

As a black man or a mixed-raced man or a mixed-heritage man or a 'person of colour', I've faced challenges from all sides. There have been occasions when black artists have thrown insults at me, questioning my identity, suggesting that I'm not 'black enough', while white colleagues have su-su'd pon me to advance their own causes or positions in the industry. Then you get the likes of Noel Gallagher dismissing black music by coming out with crap like, 'Sorry, but Jay-Z? Fucking no chance. Glastonbury has a tradition of guitar music, do you know what I mean?' Of course, by 'guitar music', what he meant was 'white music'. While black artists can have carte blanche, well, almost, to tackle any subject they please, the few senior black execs in the industry are virtually gagged from saying anything too contentious. Being one of the very few black executives in my position may have added an extra layer of uniqueness to my experience, but it also meant I had a practically non-existent lobby.

Before I got to America, I had a reasonable understanding of the racial interplay between the various ethnic groups vying for a piece of the American Dream. You had to have been living under a rock for the past 400 years not to know where the tensions between blacks and whites stemmed from; but there were other historical 'beefs' that required more understanding, especially when it came to navigating the music, media, film, sports and entertainment industries, where a lot of talent is black, and a significant number of people in key positions are Jewish.

In Britain, we like to pride ourselves on being 'tolerant', 'accepting' and 'multicultural'. As such, I was always able to have full and frank conversations with colleagues and friends about racial issues without ever feeling either the need to self-censor or mind my Ps and Qs because saying the wrong thing could wind up becoming a 'career decision'. Louis Bloom and I, for instance, would have deep conversations late into the night at Island's office in Kensington about race, and my Afro-centrism, and his Jewishness or Israel and Palestine . . . Then there was Johnny Lipsy, who moved out of London because he found the capital too anti-Semitic for his liking. He used to crack me up as, here we were, a black radical and a Jewish guy chopping it up late into the night, but always finding common ground.

In the States, however, people seemed to speak about contentious issues in ethnic silos, with blacks, whites, Jews, Hispanics and what have you never really dialoguing with each other on race. In the music industry, and elsewhere, I would find an undertone of anti-Semitism occasionally rear its head from black people who, having long seen Jewish managers, agents, record company execs, lawyers, accountants and landlords 'rip off' black people everywhere from record deals to tenancy agreements, so reasoned, thanks to the promotion of long-held bigoted views or unconscious biases, that *all* Jews were engaged in a conspiracy to rob black people blind. Patently, any right-thinking person could see that this wasn't the case, just as they wouldn't believe any of the racist tropes about black people.

* * *

The summer of 2019 saw me bag my first number one in the *Billboard* Hot 100 as head of Island US: 'Señorita' by the Canadian singer Shawn Mendes and Cuban-American singer Camila Cabello. Unlike in the UK office, where champagne corks would be popping, backs would be slapped, and high-fives would go around the room as if Harry Kane had just scored a hat-trick for England to win the World Cup, all I got were a handful of 'attaboys' and the odd fist bump. It eventually went on to break a record, topping the charts in an incredible forty countries worldwide. It also went multi-platinum in thirteen countries, including Diamond in France, Mexico and Poland. In the UK, it spent a phenomenal seven weeks at number one, charting for forty weeks in total.

Back in London, I was at Battersea Evolution for the *Music Week* Awards to pick up the Strat Award, the event's biggest accolade, one that recognises 'an outstanding contribution to the record industry'. Among the 1,300-strong crowd were musical heroes such as Led Zeppelin's Jimmy Page, and musical charges like Dizzee Rascal who, in presenting me with the award, said, 'He is a dude, man. You can just *listen* to music with him,' while Bono called me 'a prince of a man' during his touching tribute.

Being recognised as the first person of colour on the list was monumental, and it illustrated a remarkable evolution in the industry since I had entered it during that 'Second Summer of Love' in 1988, when it was far less welcoming to women and people of colour. However, current progress painted a hopeful picture for the next decade.

Throughout my journey, I'd celebrated numerous wins but also faced challenges. Moments of unwavering self-belief were occasionally overshadowed by doubt and the desire to slip back into the shadows. The Music Week Awards had always been a sanctuary for me, a space where dedication and creativity are celebrated. But despite the praise, being called a 'prince' or a 'leader', I still found myself reflecting on what leadership, and my style of it, really meant to me.

But every now and again something would come at me, left-field, as a reminder to keep it humble.

Not long after picking up the Strat, I was at an Island US party at the 1 Hotel in West Hollywood when I ran into the rapper and producer, Rodney Jerkins.

'Darcus, you need to come with me, man. I got someone here who you've just got to meet.'

As Rodney led me through the crowd, we turned a corner and there, sitting in a comfy chair, was the former undisputed heavyweight champion of the world, Mike Tyson. Rodney knew I was a fan, but I tried to play it cool.

'Hey, Mike,' beamed Rodney, 'this is Darcus, this is the guy I was telling you about. He's massive fan. He's seen every one of your fights, man. He knows what round you knocked all your opponents out in. He's . . .'

'Whoa, Rodney,' I said, leaning in. 'That's too much. I'm not that much of a fan. Don't set me up!'

Mike looked up at us, glass-eyed, staring not at me but through me. It was like I wasn't even there.

'Yo, Rodney, what's up with Mike?'

'Aw, man, don't worry about Mike. He's just done some shrooms.'

Legend.

To this day, my belief is that no one can take away your achievements. Even when I've doubted myself or let imposter syndrome get the better of me, I've always been sure of my contributions and our goals. I created a framework for others to excel in, and even when someone achieved greatness, it was within the structure I built. When I received the Strat Award, a video played, showcasing various artists I collaborated with. Their words spoke louder than anything I might say about myself. There's no need to proclaim your greatness; if you're doing something commendable, others will acknowledge it. In all my interviews, I often praise others and emphasise the talented team I work with. It's for others to commend you.

I've always believed in leading by example, be it through my contract decisions, signing ground-breaking artists, or offering support. Over time, if you've consistently delivered quality work, people will talk about it. You'll find few photos of me holding up gold disks or taking centre stage. Yes, there are moments when I've had to embrace the spotlight as president of Island US, but that's always been as a promotional tool for the artist's benefit, not mine. I usually stay in the background. I'm still that kid on the edge of the group of street urchins. At times, I've reflected on missed photo opportunities with renowned figures, but chasing such moments was never my priority. I recognise true greatness and understand that not everyone attains it. Instead of constantly seeking the spotlight, I prefer to let my deeds and reputation speak for me.

As I hit fifty, I started to question who my real self really was. Was it the Island Records guy, the one who's always leading from the front, or was it the person who sits on the sofa in silence, away from the limelight? For the past thirty years I'd been defined by a personal brand, an 'always-on' persona, but I found myself wondering if that's who I was at my core.

Looking back, I realised I'd been doing a lot of tap dancing, a lot of hiding the flaws and vulnerabilities. My real self would probably have been ignorant at times and made mistakes that could have cost me dearly. But in this position, you can't afford to show those weaknesses. You have to be strong, always moving forward, and never revealing your doubts. All that authenticity and 'keep it real' bullshit is an act. And eventually, like something out of *The Thing*, the fake you takes over the real you.

It's a constant struggle to find the balance between the public persona and the authentic self. Social media and public personas tend to only show life's highlights, while the struggles, the pain and the hurt are kept hidden. No one posts on Instagram that they're feeling depressed or lost.

Not unless they want to get fired.

Every other day, to clear my head as much as anything, I'd go for a run. I'd been into middle-distance running since I was a kid, and while I had breaks over the years, in terms of exercise or training, running was my discipline of choice, but it was also a way of knackering myself into a relatively good night's sleep. What with the workload, the headaches and the overstimulation, over the years I'd got into the habit of going to bed later and later yet having to get up earlier and earlier to deal with the conflicting time zones I had to communicate with on a daily. Half the time I didn't know if I was coming or going.

So, I ran and ran and ran. I was like Forest Gump. I conquered Central Park, the complete loop, and improved my personal best over 5K and 10K. *Run Darcus, run!* I was like 'Babe' Levy, the Dustin Hoffman character in *Marathon Man*, running around and around the Jacqueline Kennedy Onassis Reservoir until I was dead on my feet. *Is it safe?* Like Levy, I was literally and metaphorically on the run. I ran to shut out the trauma, the stress, the *world*. But as Island's anchor, I was trapped in the corporate American rat race relay. Day in, day out, I'd pick up the baton, run the gauntlet, cross the finishing line, collapse, get to my feet, pick up the baton, run the gauntlet, cross the finish line, collapse, get to my feet, pick up the baton. I started obsessively logging onto the exercise app Strava to keep on top of my training and beat my personal bests. Soon, however, I was getting overly competitive with myself. It was like crack. At first, my Strava graph, which shows your level of achievement, was flat. But over the weeks and months the trajectory went up and up and up. My mind was telling me that my body could handle the pace like I was still a teenager. Little did I know how much I was battering myself up, physically as well as mentally.

I had natural ability, proper natural ability, but I also had a refusal to train properly. Back in the day, I'd come up against kids that had trained properly, then I'd realise that I really didn't have the mental fortitude for it. But then, as I got older, I started trying to prove to myself that I did have the mentality for it, so I'd get up at six in the morning and go running on the streets, the park, Wimbledon Common, running and running and running to the point where I'd feel sick – I mean, literally throwing up. I tried to adopt the mentality of a professional athlete when I used to run. I ran in rain, wind, snow – whatever. In New York, my running got more intense as the stress of work and home life started to pile up. Round and round and round Central Park, I'd really push myself, daily. Even though I could feel the impact all that hard running was having on my body, I couldn't stop. It became a compulsion, almost a masochistic thrill. Running through the pain barrier to the point at which pain became the *thing* is something many runners, even casual joggers, experience. In fact, I was always struck by the ironic fate of James Fixx, whose bestseller, *The Complete Book of Running*, became the joggers' Bible, inspiring God knows how many people to take it up. The dude practically reinvented jogging. And this from a man who smoked forty a day in his youth. Then, in 1984, aged fifty-two, he dropped down dead from a heart attack while jogging in Vermont.

Even adjusting to the time difference took me over a year. It wasn't merely overcoming jet lag, it was about syncing with a new rhythm. Your body has to recalibrate when it wakes up, especially when you've spent so many years accustomed to a particular time zone and seasonal patterns. Transitioning to the American pace after living most of my life in London, not to mention further adjusting to New York's tempo while dealing with a constant round of transatlantic flights, was tiring enough. I then had to balance this with a new work culture on top of social and political events unfolding in America, as well as the usual soap opera of home life. Some might accuse me of belly-aching. After all, I was being handsomely remunerated for being the CEO of a globally recognised brand. But without going down the 'money can't buy you happiness' route, does money *really* buy you anything other than the same shit with a more expensive label or the 'freedom' to navigate your way through life's challenges with a little added comfort or ease?

When you go to America, or a country with that much scale, the dough becomes crazy. That's why people are so mad in America. You can literally go from zero to life-changing super-rich with the stroke of a pen. That's the American Dream. Meanwhile, in the UK, there's no real dream because there's always a ceiling, and that's before the Inland Revenue takes half of your income and you're left holding a pay cheque saying, 'Oh, man,' like you just trod in a pile of dog shit. In the UK you can make £100,000. In America, the equivalent gig nets you $2 million. That's the difference: the size, the scale, and thus the earning potential, is next level. When I went to America, shit, I was earning more than the President of the United States.

Coming from where I come from, getting to where I got to in the music industry in America was like something out of Hollywood. The rooms and houses and studios that you're in and out of are unbelievable. There I am, little Darcus Beese from west London, craning my neck looking up at skyscrapers in the Big Apple that touch the hem of St Peter. Yeah, I'm a caporegime for the 'family' that made Bob Marley and U2, Trump is on news every five minutes talking some shit, and there are top TV shows being filmed on the next street. Damn. It was like living on the set of a movie. Unlike the movies, however, I didn't get twenty takes to make a ten-second scene look perfect. Underlying all the glitz and the glamour, I knew it was one strike and you're out.

For the first year, life in New York was super-hard for Alison. But once she got into the day-to-day detail of life, familiarised herself with the neighbourhood and made some friends from Darcus's nearby school, she was all good. Or so I thought.

As we lived on the Upper West Side, which was just two stops on the subway from my office, during the day I would pop home for an hour or two, or else I would try to get home early evening.

To be brutally honest, Alison and I kept ourselves to ourselves for the most part. Young Darcus had way more friends than we did. He was out and about, socialising all the time, but we weren't. As much as I referred to New York as 'home', I just wasn't interested in making American friends. There were maybe one or two people, like Lauren Schneider – an amazing woman who was EVP, Strategic Media Relations – but other than that, I wasn't really looking to expand my social circle.

We chose to live in the city because I wanted to be close to HQ. Had I been thinking about the long term, we might have rented a house in Brooklyn or Jersey. The original plan was to spend our first year in the city to acclimatise, and then consider relocating to the suburbs. My primary concern was my job satisfaction, and I let that guide our living situation. In retrospect, maybe if we'd settled into a more permanent neighbourhood, with actual next-door neighbours instead of a revolving door of transient business-people, things might have felt more like home.

But then, the pandemic struck.

Suddenly we were all baking banana bread, seeing friends clapping for the NHS on their mobiles, watching the death toll rise, scanning endless, meaningless, scaremongering data, laughing, crying, raving in the sitting room to DJs spinning tunes in their bedrooms in far-flung places. It was all about home schooling, bigots hating on the Chinese, Zoom meetings, food deliveries, face masks, to vax or not to vax, jogging and jogging and more fucking jogging.

When America went into lockdown, I had been living there for just over a year. And lockdown in New York was no joke. COVID hit the city hard and fucked everything up. As we were bound by our tenancy agreement, we couldn't move. By the time our lease ended, many had already left the city. Essentially, we missed our window of opportunity. Timing was everything.

The government response to the pandemic in New York started with a full lockdown between March and April with myriad restrictions coming into force. Theatres, music venues and nightclubs closed; restaurants were restricted to takeaways and food deliveries only; schools gyms and sports clubs closed too. You couldn't fly, you couldn't travel, you couldn't do shit. I felt like Snake Plissken in *Escape from New York.*

We all know the script. We were all there. So I really don't want to give the pandemic any more shine than it deserves. Suffice it to say that 2020 was about to become the first of many *anni horribiles* for a whole lot of people, me included.

13

Capitalism Gone Mad

You got to be a millionaire
Or some kind of petit-bourgeoisie
Any time you living here
In this country

– Mighty Sparrow[1]

ABC NEWS, 24 JANUARY: A Michigan man has filed a lawsuit against a Midwest banking chain this week, accusing it of racial profiling, after a teller called the police on him and wrongfully accused him of fraud.

Ironically, Sauntore Thomas was attempting to deposit two large checks that he'd received as part of a workplace racial discrimination settlement with his previous employer when a TCF Bank branch in Livonia, Michigan, refused to accept the checks, saying they weren't legit.

---

[1] Slinger Francisco; Charlie's Records.

Welcome to America, 2020.

By the time we had entered lockdown in March, it was clear that work, living and travel were going to be severely dented. Doing business was one thing, however my main concern was Darcey, who, living in the UK, was now marooned from us in New York.

Despite the challenges I had as a kid, I can't help but feel relieved that I came of age when I did. The pressures kids face nowadays are immense, and they're constantly comparing themselves to others. My daughter was having a really tough time during the lockdown, as were many her age. She had changed her plans and was supposed to come and study in the US so she could be close to the family, but COVID-19 put paid to all that.

I could not only see the pandemic putting a strain on Darcey, but from talking to other parents and, crucially, witnessing young people's behaviour, I could tell it was mentally draining for the legions of kids who were turning to their mobiles and social media as a distraction from what was going on in the world. Being so glued to their mobiles, they soon started suffering from 'FOMO' and needed to be doing whatever it was they saw everyone else was doing, no matter how facile this may've seemed to us old farts. Whether it was not having the right sneakers or not having the right hairdo, or, yes, not listening to the right drill artists or bands, the sense of failing to measure up, which social media managed to put into overdrive during the pandemic, was immense.

Even before the pandemic hit, taking a simple picture with Darcey was a long, drawn-out process. She literally had to approve anything I wanted to post online of us together. Posting without her permission simply wasn't worth the aggro. If she found out – and she would because she would constantly monitor my feeds – she'd absolutely lose it. And it's not just about taking a picture;

it's about getting everything just right – the angle, the lighting, no one blinking . . . I think one of the major issues for kids today is not knowing what they want to do, and it takes a huge toll on them mentally. Kids constantly compare themselves to others and feel like they're failing because they see these seemingly perfect lives on Instagram and elsewhere and think everyone else is 'making it' and they're not. It's a lot of pressure.

Despite often being called the 'coolest man in the room' at events like the *Music Week* Awards, and admittedly having a 'thing' about my own appearance (did I mention the importance of having a proper sneaker game?), I did wonder if this obsession with appearance and aesthetics was healthy. And it wasn't just affecting kids. The highly stylised, visualised nature of modern culture meant adults were becoming more and more obsessed with how they looked, how they sounded, where they ate, drank and went on holiday. Nowadays, it seems like everything has to be just right, and even the slightest imperfection can be a cause for concern. People are so critical of themselves, nit-picking every detail.

It's the same with artists. Nowadays, they can literally make money from just a fifteen-second clip. You don't even need a full song. It's all about that catchy hook. With platforms like TikTok, it's those fifteen seconds that matter. So now, artists can earn from just a single chord, which is crazy, but also puts pressure on them to work their social media presence hard, which, just like young fans, can give them an inferiority complex if they're not earning from it. With everyone so conscious of their image and feeling the need for perfection, the music industry faces a challenge trying to connect with people in today's world.

From the moment Darcey was born in 1999, I knew I had to sort my shit out. Ditto when my son Darcus was born in 2005.

Whether it was getting a call in New York from Alison to tell me that Darcey had just taken her first steps or taking a call from her while stuck in an airport somewhere to tell me that Darcus Jr had just cut his first tooth, I was more often than not in relentless work mode at these key points in their lives. It was hard. If I wasn't under pressure to sign acts, I was under pressure to get more records out of the door, and when I wasn't doing that, the onus was on dropping artists; and so it went on, an endless cycle of signing, recording and dropping acts, which only intensified in the States. I'd gone from running at 100mph as head of Island UK to running 200mph as the boss of Island US.

Over the years, I'd get home after an exhausting day, but still be in work mode for *hours*, as I'd often have a series of international conference calls to make. Not having come from a world of 'Hi, kids, Daddy's home. Let's spend three hours of quality time together!', that just wasn't happening. I didn't have the presence of mind, or the familial benchmark from my own upbringing, to act any differently. I felt my just being there was something in itself because of how little my father was around for me. But there's more to parenting than simply being in the room. Getting stuck in an endless loop of naked ambition was starting to take its toll. I was reaching a point where it wasn't even about a desperate need for success. I just didn't want to *fail*. And not wanting to fail felt like a copout.

As soon as COVID hit – and I know many millions of people went through the same thing – life just caught up with me. Where, previously, I'd never had time to think, now it was like I had all the time in the world. Everything just stopped and for the first time in decades, I had time to reflect – more than enough time. My ambition was trying to get the family to where it needed to be so that we could be financially secure, but in doing so you're at risk of ending up with a wreckage of a family. Once I started to take stock, I realised, *Shit*, there was some stuff that I missed out on and took for granted.

Lockdown also saw me smoking more weed. I'd been a smoker since my teens, and it had become a habitual way for me to slow down, otherwise I'd be climbing up the walls. When people would say, 'Darcus, how can you smoke weed?' I'd be like, 'How can you drink beer?' Having never been a big drinker, thanks to seeing the effect it had on my parents, a pint of lager or a glass of wine would send me sideways. Because weed was practically on tap in New York, and because I was often in LA, where *everybody* smokes weed, I found myself puffing more than usual.

'You really need to stop,' my doctor told me during a routine check-up.

'Why?'

'Darcus, because you're over fifty. How many of your friends still smoke?

'Not many. Probably just me and my mate Clive, right?'

'Why did your other friends stop smoking?'

'Because they just couldn't handle it anymore,' I said, wondering where this interrogation was going. 'Because they all got old, and they couldn't handle it anymore, and it made them paranoid, and blah, blah, blah . . .'

'Do you think that cannabis might be having the same effect on you?'

'Yeah, probably. Probably. No, definitely!'

I tried to laugh it off, but the doctor was right. I had to cut down on smoking. Smoking, for me, was like social media is for kids, an addictive distraction, a form of escapism that took me away from the reality of life for black people in America. I could get stoned in my little bubble and disappear in a cloud of smoke as every time I looked at my social media, turned on the TV news, or picked up a newspaper, there seemed to be yet another extrajudicial killing of a black person, usually a young male. It would always send shivers down my spine.

Just before America went into lockdown, there came the first of what felt like a genocidal spike in police killings of black people, but on reflection was simply just the latest iteration of a 400-year culture of white supremacy.

The 'season of goodwill' had barely ended in God-fearing America when, on 23 February, Ahmaud Arbery, a young black man who was just going about his business, just out jogging in a 'white neighbourhood' near his home in Georgia, was shot dead by three white men. Why? Because they 'suspected' he was a burglar, a suspicion based on nothing more than the colour of his skin. That's the summit of white privilege for you: the 'right' to take the law into your own hands and kill black people, often with impunity. It took two months for the authorities to arrest the men responsible for killing Ahmaud, even though police knew within minutes of his fatal shooting who the suspects, or, as they referred to them at the time, 'witnesses', were.[2]

---

[2] A federal judge sentenced two Georgia men to life imprisonment on 8 August for the pursuit and slaying of Ahmaud Arbery; a third man was sentenced to thirty-five years. A jury had determined that the three white men – Travis McMichael, thirty-six; his father, Gregory McMichael, sixty-six; and their neighbour, William Bryan, fifty-two – were motivated by racism when they chased Mr Arbery, a 25-year-old black man, through their neighbourhood. They were each convicted of a federal hate crime.

Not long after breaking into the music industry, I had seen the LAPD's infamous 1991 Rodney King beating. It was arguably the forerunner to today's social media examples of extrajudicial violence, given the impact that video had on racial tensions in America and the protracted rioting that followed the acquittal of King's assailants, which resulted in sixty-three deaths, 2,383 injuries, a staggering 12,000-plus arrests and over $1 billion in property damage. The policing of black people before and after the LA riots was connected to law enforcement's siege mentality, in part stemming from policing one of America's largest gang crime areas, but also driven by a historic fear, and hatred, of black people dating back to the Watts riots of 1965, which in turn owes much to the post-war Second Great Migration, which saw large numbers of black people head west in search of work and a better life but unsurprisingly saw this new influx ghettoised due to LA's racist housing policies.

That 'melting pot' of course laid the foundation for the Bloods and the Crips gangs, and the West Coast gangsta rap phenomenon, which in its own uncompromising, graphic, X-rated style was a form of protest movement, albeit one that was underscored by a lot of nihilism.

Like countless parents, I feared for my children every time they stepped out of the front door. And as a black father, I was particularly concerned about the dangers of knife crime and gang culture that my teenaged son faced, be it New York or London. Adding to these anxieties, however, there was a heightened concern about how law enforcement treated young men of colour, and potential prejudices from white neighbours, something that I was no stranger to in the UK but in the US was off the hook. Amid all this, I was presented with a choice: to stay or to leave.

Staying was tempting because of the financial incentives, and I genuinely enjoyed my life in America. However, the decision became more complicated when I considered the political climate during Trump's tenure and the degree to which white police, and white members of the public period, were seemingly able to kill young black men and people of colour with impunity.

It got to the point where I could reel off the names of black people who'd been killed by the police or 'concerned' white citizens in the US at the drop of a hat – even before I'd moved to New York. Philando Castile, Eric Garner, Michael Brown, Breonna Taylor, Ahmaud, Tamir Rice . . . these were people, just like me, shot dead while going about their business, in their own neighbourhoods and homes, or, in the case of twelve-year-old Tamir, while playing with a toy gun.

Once again, I was questioning my own identity, not existentially, but in the context of the role I now had as a global cultural gatekeeper. In the UK, I'd been walking a fine line on race all my life. Mum and Dad were in the Black Panthers, and I'd always felt proud to be black. In fact, I always made a point of playing James Brown's 'Say It Loud, I'm Black and I'm Proud' to my kids, but when Alison and I finally got together, she had a one-and-a-half-year-old blond-haired blue-eyed son, which was a challenge, given the pressure that multicultural families face beyond the fantasy world of a Waitrose Christmas commercial.

Where does pride in one's nature end and nationalism, jingoism or outright racism begin? In the highly charged arena of race in America, I had no choice but to view life through a far more racialised lens, and that meant reflecting on things like what black women think about my relationship with Alison, even when viewed from a distance on the street or while out shopping or socialising. As I felt more under the spotlight in America, perhaps I was inclined to do a lot of overthinking. But there's no escaping the fact that race is way more political in America than in the UK. That's not to say that I've ever had an issue with being in a mixed-race relationship, or 'marrying out'. However, I recognise it might be for others because of prevailing perceptions. It's something you can't change, so I tried not to let it bother me. With people running around in MAGA caps toting AR-15s at black kids, Obama and the promise of a post-racial America seemed like a dream turned nightmarish. That's why I always reminded my children that no matter how much they identify as mixed-race or biracial, society primarily sees them as black. Regardless of their light skin, if the situation arose, and it's an extreme thought, they won't be lumped in with the whites: they're getting thrown in the truck with the rest of us niggers.

I was deeply concerned about my son's interactions with the public and the police, especially as I was being deluged with viral videos of 'Karens' or police officers in heated or violent confrontations with black people on the street, at school, in shopping malls – everywhere. It felt as though, in Trump's America, many white people – civilian or otherwise – had regressed to a Wild West, frontier-settler mentality. It was crazy to think, but the reality was, if you were black, getting stopped by the police or encountering a trigger-happy white person having a bad day greatly increased your chances of being shot dead. As a black father, I was acutely aware that if my son was skating around New York with his schoolmates, sporting a big Afro and a Black Lives Matter T-shirt, he could easily be a target. He often skated in areas where the police might ask him to leave, increasing the chances of a minor incident escalating – with potentially dire consequences.

When I first got to America, I was full of the American Dream, sky's the limit, the world is your oyster and all that bullshit. And why wouldn't I be? When I was coming up in the UK, not only were the doors closed, they'd also have a foot pressed against them, as well as being padlocked and bolted. In America, however, if you have an entrepreneurial spirit and the work ethic, no one can tell you jack. Anyone can end up being one of the most powerful people in the world. Again, it's not a cliché. Facebook started in a dorm. Def Jam started in a dorm. The real challenge in this game is making it to a decade and beyond. When you get to fifteen, twenty years, that's making it. Because everything's a flash in a pan these days. Three or five years, that's just one or two cycles of things – that's a football player's contract. I have seen people, and artists, come and go. Often, they've had some major success, and I'm like, 'Cool. Trust me: I won't see you again.'

Operating on a full tank allows you to handle these challenges more effectively. Even though some situations remain tough, you can manage them. Previously, those challenges wouldn't have been overwhelming. Being in America was different. For all the opportunity, the resources and blue-sky thinking, the bosses there didn't understand me the way they did in the UK. They managed me differently than how I would've been managed back home. My management approach was the same, and it's a two-way street. But being Afro-Caribbean in America is different from being African-American. I was starting to seriously question if I'd made enough progress to feel valuable in the US.

There I was, living in an apartment on the Upper West Side, in a bubble. It was virtually unheard of for someone to transition from where I'd grown up in London to wind up where I was now. I could genuinely lay claim to being the hero of my very own rags-to-riches story. But the perfect shit storm had started to brew in America; my daughter not being with me, work becoming more stressful, my anxiety rising and the 'dream' feeling unsustainable. Everything had started to layer up. On one shoulder, there was that little imp saying, 'Fuck it. Just carry on taking the dough.' On the other shoulder, the angel of my better nature would say, 'Bro, this isn't *real*. This isn't *you*.' At some point, I had to decide what I was going to do: stay and get paid more dough than I'd ever seen before in my life, or don't get paid.

I can't speak for everybody in that creative space, but, for me, I just needed something more. Having thought as a kid that getting record tokens for Christmas was the golden ticket, as someone from my background, cut from a different cloth, coming from the UK, to make it in the American music industry? Damn. Now I really was Charlie in the Chocolate Factory. But some things just didn't sit well with me. How rich was I prepared to get? Could it be at the expense of my health, my family cohesion, my diaspora? Many in the pressure cooker of corporate America get over such internal conflicts by just taking more pills and medicating their way through the philosophical pain barrier.

In America, money is king. I counted myself lucky because I'd reached a point where I had enough financial freedom to bail out. I'm not trying to be worthy and suggest that money didn't matter. Of course it did. After all, I'd worked my way up from rags to riches, and I certainly wasn't going back to rags. But at some point, my better angel couldn't stop asking, 'What is right – for me, for my health and my family?' At what point do you start talking truth to yourself? What difference did another million really make? None, unless I was going to spend it. Did prioritising my mental health mean more to me than earning a shitload of money? Don't get me wrong, I thought making a lot of money was great. But there came a point when I had to consider my wellbeing. I felt a profound, deep unhappiness within my soul. Sure, I could afford better therapy and medications, but when does such a lifestyle become untenable? Some of the darkest moments during my time in America came when I was 'in season' and suffering from cluster headaches. When it came along there was no way I could survive without my medication. When I first got to New York, for instance, I ran out of medication after my supply got trapped in customs for an inordinate amount of time. I completely lost my shit. Just to get a sense of normalcy from the resulting injection felt like a high, such was the pain, which I'd come to see as a dark monster living inside my head, caged but clawing to get out through my left eye or through the back of my neck. As soon as I felt that aura coming, I'd grab my pen, load up, twist, stab and inject it into my inner thigh. The next five to seven minutes would feel like hell, but then the pain would recede and the intoxicating sensation of having a clear head would waft over me as the monster was put back behind bars. Still, at least I wasn't living in medieval times when the slightest mention of monsters or demons in my head would've got me burned at the stake.

Dealing with a lot of shit when you're healthy is hard enough; and a lot of shit was what I had to deal with in New York. Work, home and daily life became increasingly stressful, not just because of the inherent challenges that, say, renegotiating an artist's contract might bring, or battling with the condo committee because your neighbours don't like the sweet smell of marijuana wafting out of your apartment through the airducts into their boudoirs, but because New York is, even by American standards, a neurotic city. When you have, for instance, at one end of the spectrum, someone coming crying to you after getting triggered by the colour of their colleague's furniture, and at the other end, a genuine fear that a cop might shoot your son dead for scooting around Central Park in a Black Lives Matter t-shirt, the stress gets really dialled up when you realise that you're not in remission and your lifestyle may well be contributing to rattling your inner monster's cage. As I didn't have a US doctor, at one stage I found myself almost out of medication and probably two, maybe three injections away from my head exploding. Fortunately, my re-up came through customs just in the nick of time, but not before my body started to feel like it was folding in on me.

One day, I caught myself doing a double take in the mirror, the way you do when you feel like you're looking at a completely different person. C'mon . . . you *know* that feeling. You stare at yourself, at the wrinkles, the grey hair, the sunken eyes, and you know something's not right. I wasn't looking at me. I was looking at what I'd become, and what I'd become wasn't healthy. Still, I deluded myself, as you do when you push through any pain barrier, that I could take it. Heart- and lungs-wise, I thought I was healthy. But my mind and overall body were breaking down. Beyond the first year in New York when I was pumped up and fighting fit, the relentlessness of the Big Apple, the unsustainability of my diary, the painkillers all conspired to drag me down into the deep waters of lockdown. I could feel myself going under, but denial would push me back up above the surface just long enough to take in a gulp of air to stop myself from drowning.

Working from home seemed to exacerbate the headaches. But I'd come to accept the headaches, the stress and the gradual breaking down of my mind and body as an occupational hazard. I'd go to bed in pain and wake up in pain. How was this possible? When you're asleep you're not doing anything. I kept up with my running despite it being agonising because I *needed* to run, because I had become addicted to pain, because I thought this is *it*, this is what success looks like: being constantly on the verge of a mental and physical breakdown. I'd pop more pills, smoke more dope, take more injections when the headaches came. I'd Zoom, call, email all the hours God sent, go to bed, wake up again in pain and start all over again. Seven days a week.

In America, there's the drive to be successful and the drive to be rich, but you never knew when enough was enough. And enough is *never* enough in America. As Tony Montana said of his own fateful American Dream in *Scarface*, 'I want what's coming to me [. . .] the world, and everything in it.' In fact, right across American popular culture, from *Citizen Kane* to Ice Cube's ironic payoff at the end of 'It Was a Good Day', anyone chasing the American Dream either comes to a tragic or very sticky end. I saw it with my own eyes: contemporaries would get richer and richer, buy bigger and bigger houses, then start living beyond their financial, physical and emotional means to maintain the façade. For me, with nearly three years under my belt in New York, I could feel myself getting ready to tap out.

14

Fight the Power

Our freedom of speech is freedom or death
We got to fight the powers that be

                          – Public Enemy[1]

The morning of 25 May 2020 was just another pandemic Monday. After my usual run around Central Park, I got home, got my shit together and logged onto Zoom for the first of an endless round of video conferences, telephone calls and other virtual comms. The office had been shut down for several weeks, and like countless hundreds of millions of people the world over, I was now working from home – or indeed often not working at all – with no prospect of a return to normality in sight. There we were, in our little online boxes, some completely locked down and unable to leave their homes, others free to go for a walk, or a swim, or a run, but all of us going slightly mad.

---

[1] Carlton Ridenhour, Eric Sadler, Hank Boxley, Keith Boxley; Motown.

No sooner had I sat down at my desk than I noticed that Facebook and Twitter were blowing up with a bizarre video clip: a testy encounter had gone down that morning between a black male birdwatcher named Christian Cooper and a white female dog walker called Amy Cooper (no relation) in a section of Central Park just a stone's throw from my apartment. The clip, which was shot by the birdwatcher, had recorded the woman (who soon earned the nickname 'Central Park Karen') saying to the birdwatcher, 'I'm calling the cops . . . I'm gonna tell them there's an African-American man threatening my life', having been asked, politely, to leash her dog, as was required in that part of the park.

There have been times in America's violent history that such an encounter would've gotten the birdwatcher lynched. In 1955, for instance, fourteen-year-old Emmett Till was abducted, tortured and lynched in Mississippi for the alleged 'crime' or 'offending' a white woman. The woman, Carol Bryant, had accused young Emmett of wolf-whistling at her. Getting wind of this, Bryant's then-husband and his half-brother murdered Emmett, a crime they were acquitted of by an all-white jury but nevertheless later admitted to in a *Look* magazine interview, such was the impunity they knew their white privilege extended to. (Oddly, lynching would not become a federal hate crime until President Joe Biden signed it into law in 2022.)

In the UK, we've long had our own issues with racially motivated killings. A couple of years before Dad emigrated to Britain, and three years after Emmett Till's death, a 32-year-old Antiguan named Kelso Cochrane was murdered by a gang of white boys. No one was ever convicted, not least because of the Met Police's complacency. Kelso's killing led to Trinidadian journalist and civil rights activist Claudia Jones organising a series of cultural events that helped to eventually catalyse the Notting Hill Carnival – another case of the black experience finding a voice in music culture. Then, of course, there was Bangladeshi textile worker Altab Ali, whose racist murder Mum and I protested over in the summer of 1978. Then in 1993 came one of the UK's most infamous racist killings, that of black teenager Stephen Lawrence, in Eltham, southeast London, again by a gang of white boys, again with another dubious investigation by the Met, which eventually led to the disgraced police force being deemed 'institutionally racist' by the 1998 Macpherson report before, in 2012, two of the original five suspects in the case were finally convicted of Stephen's murder.

In the three decades since, and before, Stephen's death, there have been several unsolved or poorly prosecuted murders of black and brown Britons, immigrants, asylum seekers and refugees. We have had our fair share of race hate crimes and examples of police brutality, but in America, it is completely scaled up.

I'd only ever associated Minneapolis, Minnesota, with being the birthplace of one of my musical heroes: Prince. But when, in the early hours of 26 May, a ten-minute-and-nine-second Facebook video emerged of a black man being choked to death, in real time, by a white police officer the previous evening, suddenly Minneapolis became synonymous with two words: George Floyd.

Unless you've been living on a another planet since 2020, you know the story. I don't need to go there other than to say George Floyd's murder by Derek Chauvin and the words 'I can't breathe' reverberated around the world as American racism was laid bare for all to see. Of course, this wasn't the first time the police had been caught on camera wilfully killing black people. And, alas, it won't be the last.

In 2020, around 1,159 people lost their lives in encounters with the police. Among them, 287 were black. The following year would see even more black Americans killed by police – 305 out of 1,147. In 2022, US police killed more people than they had in a decade, around 1,197. Black people accounted for 26 per cent, or 313, of those killed. At the time of writing, 61 of the 363 killed by police in America were black.[2] In the year George Floyd was killed, police officers got off scot-free in 270 killings of black people. Only those involved in thirteen cases were charged.

No one is suggesting that police officers don't have a tough job to do, nor that they shouldn't have the right to defend themselves and the public against hostile suspects – regardless of colour. Living in America during the pandemic, I often found myself disappearing down a rabbit hole of livestreamed, mobile-recorded and caught-on-bodycam 'officer-involved shootings' videos. If lockdown provided us all with plenty of time to perfect our tinpot drumming skills, overnight oats recipes and armchair virological expertise, it also gave a shitload of algorithms the chance to fill our social media with endless images of the state in conflict with the people and vice versa. I've seen enough viral videos of seemingly compliant people turn on police, and suddenly produce a knife or gun, or disarm a cop, before going on to attack them or random members of the public, to know that sometimes deadly force is the only option. But I've also seen plenty of clips where trigger-happy cops or mob-handed officers shoot or choke out an innocent black person for no good reason, other than the obvious: racism.

---

[2] May 2023.

The history of racism and systemic oppression in the country has left a profound impact on the African-American community, and it continues to be a significant struggle even for successful black people. As Malcolm X once said of black people being stopped and harassed by the police, 'You might be a doctor, a lawyer, a preacher, or some other kind of Uncle Tom. But despite your professional standing, you'll find that you're the same victim as the man who's in the alley.' But social status aside, the extent to which race and racism are interwoven into every layer of American society is lost on most people, even Americans.

Thanks to its thriving popular culture, of which music is a core thread, it's easy to forget that for all the posturing in the Declaration of Independence that 'all men are created equal' and are 'endowed by their Creator with certain unalienable Rights', among them 'Life, Liberty and the pursuit of Happiness', America was built on the back of slavery, fought a civil war over it, assassinated a President over it, and eventually gave rise to an apartheid regime whose legacy can be seen across the country in the form of Confederate statues, flags and, worst still, policies and practices that ought to shame the nation but nonetheless underpinned the election of Donald Trump. Perhaps I was naïve to think otherwise, or was simply ignorant of the facts, but for an African-American, seeing the Confederate flag flying over his statehouse or having to pass a statue of Robert E. Lee every day on the way to work was like a German Jew seeing a swastika flying over the capital of his *bundesländer* or a bronze of Hitler outside his local *untergrundbahn* station. Such a situation, quite rightly, would not only be incomprehensible, it would be illegal, yet 44 million black Americans must endure such ritual humiliations alongside a daily grind of micro and macro aggressions that suggest that America has a long way to go when it comes to 'race relations'.

As soon as I became president of Island US and gained a much higher profile, I had to be way more careful about what I said. I'd gone from being a semi-private citizen operating out of a familial office in west London to being a 'public figure' based in NYC, capital city of the world. And despite the tumult of material I came across daily on social media, which pointed to a society in the throes of a mass nervous breakdown, I had to stay away from sharing serious opinions online, not just my everyday thoughts, feelings, and observations of the world, but specifically, my attitude towards America. I now had to think twice before hitting send on a critical email, sardonic tweet or OTT Instagram post. If you wanted to hear my *serious* opinion on anything, we'd have to sit down for a *real* conversation. My heartfelt feelings, at such an incendiary time, weren't something I could just throw out there casually. I knew my opinions might not sit well with a lot of people, especially regarding how I perceive the world and how I knew the world perceives me. In a nutshell, I couldn't be *me*.

As a black CEO and president of a major business, I was even more conspicuous. Island was doing something in the region of $150 million in annual revenue in the US as part of a Universal Music Group empire that at the last count had turned over some $3.5 billion. Yet, despite my position, the stakes, the dough, the shareholders, America – Jesus, the *world* – had just witnessed a real-time lynching. As the sun came up on the Land of the Free the next day, the trauma in black America was just off the scale. *Everyone* was talking about it on the phone, on the radio, on TV, on Twitter, Facebook, Instagram, YouTube, in closed

WhatsApp groups . . . I felt a responsibility to talk to the team, via Zoom. It was tense.

There was much black anger in the room, and much white guilt. Both emotions were palpable, both vocally on screen and in off-the-record phone calls that were made to me, particularly by black members of staff. But the anger, without doubt, was most palpable on the streets of America. By conservative estimates, the Black Lives Matter protests that came in the wake of George Floyd's death attracted more than 26 million Americans in 2,000 cities and towns in every state in the United States, making it the most widespread protest movement (centred on a single issue) in the nation's history. By the end of June alone, one month into the protests, 14,000 people had been arrested. Despite the pandemic and lockdown restrictions on people's movements (or perhaps because of these), the reverberation from George's death generated protests that continued in some cities for four months solid, finally coming to an end in September 2020.

During the Black Lives Matter movement, many companies were doing Tuesday blackouts and making big statements about standing with black communities. I found it odd that they suddenly felt the need to make such statements. It's like they weren't supporting black people before. Companies that had previously been silent on equality, diversity and inclusion, or 'EDI', now had to hold the mirror up and admit that they were behind in diversity. Black people were underrepresented in many companies, mine included, so like many high-profile organisations during this soul-searching, fractious period, Universal created a task force in response to the groundswell of anger spreading across America – an America, which, if you watch too much TV or listened to too much Donald Trump, was 'literally' going up in flames.

Entitled the 'Task Force for Meaningful Change', TFMC was designed to become a 'driving force for equality and social justice'. Backed by a $25 million fund, the idea was that TFMC would be a space within the company where people, specifically black people, in the company could really voice their concerns and their anger, some of it historical, and some of it real-time.

Having been in the inner circle and seen the behind-the-scenes workings of the industry, I knew exactly how things really were. I had been part of discussions aimed at promoting diversity and come to realise much of the talk was just that: talk. Actions speak louder than words, and there was so much more to be done. Sitting on the task force, though, I soon realised that the moment I piped up with an opinion or feedback, all I heard were crickets, all I saw was tumbleweed rolling off into the distance. The silence was deafening. I was left thinking, *Oh, shit. I'm not African-American.* My experience was not their experience. As this was BLM's time, all the talk about 'black leadership' and 'black empowerment' and 'black lives' really meant 'African-American'. This was all about their trajectory, not mine. Coming from the UK, despite being a black man, my skin colour didn't matter. What mattered was that I was not a black American, which introduced me to, as Amy would've put it, a whole new level of 'fuckery'. Intra-racial politics, and the rise of African-American cultural imperialism in the US in fact got so messed up that black Americans went on the rampage against Adele for sporting Bantu knots and a Jamaican flag bikini in celebration of that summer's cancelled Notting Hill Carnival, accusing her of 'cultural appropriation' while Jamaicans themselves and the Caribbean diaspora, for the most part, showed her love for representing the community with a tongue-in-cheek look. And Americans claim that they *do* get irony? Do me a favour.

People would say to me, *without* a hit of irony, 'What, you got black people in the UK?' It was that kind of madness, ignorance and cultural alienation I'd experienced as a kid being called a 'nigger' in a white Britain and mocked as being a 'red man' in black Trinidad. All I could think was that, despite the brutality, abuse of power and racism of the UK's police and criminal justice system, from the Mangrove Nine to multiple deaths in custody, disproportionate sentences and riot provocations, no matter how bad *we* thought we had it, America's racist criminal justice industrial complex was on another level. This made black America as inward-looking and parochial as white America, which, when I voiced a counterintuitive or non-aligned view, made me sound, given my executive position, perhaps, like I was exerting a privilege that black Americans don't have, or maybe choose not to exert. Maybe, as I had demonstrated throughout my life, it was easier to tell a white man to 'go fuck yourself' when you knew the chances of having your head blown off were way slimmer in the UK than in the US.

That said, what I saw happening to my African-American cousins was a painful reminder of how disenfranchised black people were in Britain, too. While I was far less likely to be shot dead while jogging around Hyde Park than in Central Park, thanks to a legacy of colonialism, indentured labour and of course slavery, white supremacy was as much part of the black–white power dynamic in Britain as it was in any country where the colonised and the coloniser had to 'get over it' and 'tolerate' each other. But when it came to resolving the legacy of slavery, where was the value in being tolerated? In America, the scene of the crime that was slavery is America, as much as it is in the Atlantic that slaves drowned during crossing and the African nations from where millions of people were stolen during three centuries of human trafficking. In Britain, however, but for a minority of African servants whom British aristocrats and merchants 'imported' from their plantations in the New World, slavery was out of sight and out of mind, which conveniently gets many Brits off the hook today, and why they can't understand the motives behind protestors wanting to rip down statues and monuments that commemorate former slave owners.

In America, the relationship between slavery and racism is a constant dynamic. It's highly contested, it's edgy and at times violent; but at least it's an ongoing debate. In Britain, however, slavery in the Caribbean, along with the colonialism and post-Windrush immigration that followed, as well as the role these seismic historical events have played in shaping modern Britain are a source of constant discomfort for many, so much so that they'd rather pretend that none of it ever happened so that we can all 'move on'. Well, it's hard to 'move on' from a conflict without resolving it. It took me a long time to appreciate why my father fought so hard for black people to be recognised as an inclusive part of the modern British narrative as opposed to being *apart* from it, but I get it now.

Once Black Lives Matter had started to gain momentum, companies suddenly began to reflect on their diversity and make statements. Companies would say, 'We stand together with our black brothers and sisters,' but I wondered where that sentiment was the day before. Everyone rushed to show they were not racist or to express solidarity, but it felt like a reactive move. I had to bite my tongue a lot during that time because whenever I pointed out the reality that all we ever saw was one in and one out in terms of black representation, I'd get shot down.

In the years since I'd left the UK, regardless of all the EDI lip service on both sides of the Atlantic, I wish I could have been more vocal, but for all the anti-racist voices that were now being heard, mine had to stay relatively muted to avoid having a negative effect on the company's share price. That's the difference between being an associate and a godfather, a soldier and a general, a member of staff and the CEO: when you're at the bottom, you talk, people listen, they nod their head, and they ignore you. When you're at the top, all you have to do is fart and people hear an explosion, which means a *lot* of people get hurt in the crush.

It was, however, great to see artists, actors and musicians using their platforms to amplify the message of justice and equality. Just three weeks after George Floyd's death I watched Dave Chappelle's powerful Netflix special, *8:46* (broadcast on YouTube), in which the celebrated comedian used George's murder to rail against violence towards black men. Japanese-Haitian tennis star Naomi Osaka refused to play in a semi-final match of the New York Western and Southern Open in protest at George's murder. The directors of the tournament postponed all matches for that day, and when they resumed, Osaka wore a Black Lives Matter T-shirt while winning her semi-final match. She continued her support for the BLM movement later that August when she showed up at her first match at the US Open wearing a COVID-19 black mask with 'Breonna Taylor' printed in white lettering in homage to the 26-year-old, unarmed medical worker who'd been shot and killed – in her own home for fuck's sake – in Louisville, Kentucky, in March of that year.

Black American celebrities stepped into the fold with hard cash, too. Basketball legend and Charlotte Hornets owner

Michael Jordan pledged $100 million to support racial equality and social justice organisations over the next ten years. Entertainer Nick Cannon produced a George Floyd 'I Can't Breathe' video followed by a video featuring Common and John Legend, the proceeds of which went to the Floyd family and their legal team. Unlike in the UK, economies of scale meant black people could put their money where their mouths were to help effect change.

But despite achieving great success and wealth, black Americans still faced discrimination, prejudice and danger, which was deeply concerning and disheartening. George Floyd's murder at the hands of a white cop was nothing new to the black community, but it served as a moment of reckoning for America and the rest of the world.

The interplay between race and economics is a complex and multifaceted issue. Economic success doesn't automatically erase the racial barriers and challenges that black Americans face. It's not just about individual achievement, it's about the larger systemic issues that need to be addressed to bring about real change and equality. Even for someone like Will Smith, who appeared to have it all, there was immense pressure, and no escape from the myth of the black male role model. In the US and the UK, when white people have a problem, it's society's duty to fix it. But when black people have a problem, it's left to us and us alone to sort it out. Ultimately, we were all just ordinary people doing our best, and we shouldn't place unrealistic expectations on ourselves given that we have to, generally speaking, work twice as hard for half the reward.

This issue extended beyond the music industry. Many companies had to hold up a mirror and acknowledge their lack of diversity, but my perspective was that it would always be one step forward and one step back, and that was always going to be an unpopular view to express in a corporate environment controlled by rich white liberals. Throughout history, black people have faced immense challenges, often to our own detriment. Not just in the US, but throughout the diaspora, the black experience is framed by the history, impact and legacy of 400 years of transatlantic slavery. It's essential to acknowledge this without sugar-coating the past.

With the ever-expanding growth in popularity of black music, record companies felt the need to increase staffing with the appropriate experience. Before hip-hop and R&B started to dominate the charts and the Black Lives Matter movement went from strength to strength, there wasn't a significant cultural drive or appetite to properly acknowledge black people's contribution to the music industry. No one was really up in arms, even though issues persisted regarding record companies signing black artists. This was evident even during the '90s. But now, with black music becoming a mainstream economic force, and other entertainment industry campaigns such as #OscarsSoWhite changing the landscape, record companies are paying more attention. Additionally, there's now a noticeable enthusiasm among young black individuals eager to join the music industry. Previously, the interest was primarily among those already familiar with the industry. Today, given the ease with which music can be produced and shared, it seems everyone, whether they're part of a group or just close friends, is somehow involved in or drawn to the music scene. And for now, I say let's take that as progress.

I had always said that I would stay in the US for as long as I was successful. My whole five-year plan (something my father's

Windrush generation had also bargained on) was predicated on trying not to get fired. For my entire career, my whole mantra had been, 'Don't get fired!' I always felt that the way to achieve this was to be instrumental in helping artists make great records while staying relevant and being indispensable. What I hadn't accounted for were external bumps in the road, such as – oh, I don't know, a global pandemic and the rebirth of a mass African-American civil rights movement as a response to right-wing extremism and extrajudicial murder.

For the most part, we all know what true anger is, what really matters, and why we're upset. Working in the music industry shouldn't be a reason to be angry. Yes, I get frustrated if I lose a deal, or don't get the sort of deal I want, but what really makes me angry is when people lack a work ethic because they don't care. I take our work seriously because we hold people's careers and trajectories in our hands. So, my emotions might seem contradictory at times, but they all stem from a place of passion for our work and the people we work with.

And yet and yet and yet ... For all the protests, marches, demonstrations, boycotts, civil disobedience, political battles and clarion calls for justice in the wake of George Floyd's death, what had changed at the top in terms of political, institutional and corporate interests?

While governors in all but five states signed police reform laws, many of those laws conveniently gave police more protections, too. More than a dozen states only passed laws aimed at broadening police accountability; five states only passed new police protections. Meanwhile, it's been revealed that in the last decade, America's police forces have paid out more than $3.2 billion to settle claims, with many of the largest settlements going to

African-American victims of police brutality, or their families. The city of Minneapolis, for instance, agreed to pay George Floyd's family $27 million to settle a civil lawsuit.

Post-George Floyd, America is undergoing an Afrocentric renaissance that has resulted in, as African-American entrepreneur and record exec Steve Stoute calls it, 'the Tanning of America'. Urban hip-hop culture has helped redefine notions of global coolness – both on the streets and in the boardroom – which gives the impression that black America is on the up, and black culture is broadening its global cultural reach. But while the median black household in America has around $24,000 in savings, investments, home equity and other elements of wealth, the median White household has around $189,000 – a disparity that has worsened in recent decades.

The proliferation of black and biracial celebrities, sports stars, politicians and media personalities – on both sides of the Atlantic – belie economic, health and wellbeing problems that came to the fore during the pandemic but are now being swept under the carpet. As the advertising industry and big brands lurched towards equity, diversity and inclusion – and cynically used George Floyd's death and the BLM brand as their 'inspiration' – I couldn't help but question their motives and money behind the corporate sector's 'tanning' activities.

The more I got into it, the more I saw George Floyd as just the tip of a very big, very dark iceberg. What changed after Michael Brown's killing by police and the resultant riots in Ferguson, Missouri, in 2014? Riots that lasted in several waves for a whole fucking year. What about the 2018 'incident' in which a white policewoman mistakenly entered a black man's apartment thinking it was hers, and shot him dead? Another case saw a white policewoman shout, 'Taser, taser, taser,' at a black suspect, only to have, again, 'mistakenly' drawn her firearm instead, shooting the man dead.

It had been four years since former San Francisco quarter-back-cum-civil rights activist Colin Kaepernick had started taking the knee during the US national anthem in protest at police brutality. He made a statement by not bowing down to get back into the NFL. If more sports figures were like him, or Naomi Osaka, or Lewis Hamilton, or Raheem Sterling, and were willing to forgo endorsements and brand partnerships because they refuse to be seen as purely wholesome and nonpartisan, but instead as agents of change, it could make a significant difference. Ditto the music industry.

While not exactly fist-bumping or high-fiving or bro-hugging or any number of Afrocentric modes of communication that have entered mainstream global culture over the decades, taking the knee, the BLM acronym, and the name 'George Floyd' have become extended code for a way of thinking, and acting, that is redrawing the global map, not just in terms of civil and human rights, but also in terms of how blackness is viewed. George Floyd's death hit a deeper psychological nerve that went beyond the catalysation of a protest movement – and the music industry was right to respond to it. But how far could this emotional, intellectual and cultural shift go? Did it mark a rise in Afrocentrism, or an 'African renaissance' that would change the way we live, work, love and coexist? How much of a threat was all this to Eurocentrism and 'white privilege'? If the rising tide of American racism, and the far-right backlash against BLM was anything to go by, white America was in shock. The way that Colin Kaepernick and other sports stars were vilified for exerting their first-amendment right to free speech, while gun-toting white racists banged on about their second amendment right to bear arms and thus murder innocent black people, was disgusting.

It wasn't something I'd signed up for when I'd agreed to head to New York.

In the two years to date that I'd been running Island US, I'd overseen releases by Shawn Mendes, Jessie Reyez, the Killers, Skip Marley, Toni Braxton and more, and helped reshape the Island roster with a slew of new signings. I thought I was doing good things. I'd also overseen Island's year-long celebration of Bob Marley's 75th birthday in 2020, which included reissues, new recordings and a host of events and happenings. I had been named one of *Billboard*'s 'Change Agents' and gained a reputation as an 'artist-first executive', according to *Music Week*.

People often perceive the music industry as being all about fame and glamour, but trust me, it takes a lot of blood, sweat and failure to create those moments of success. Behind the scenes, it's a high-pressure environment for everyone involved, from the tea boy all the way up to the rock star. There's this constant need to deliver, and everyone has an opinion – either it's terrible or it's brilliant. Something is usually considered rubbish until it becomes a hit, or until someone with credibility vouches for it, then, suddenly, it's credible. Within much of the industry now operating from behind a Zoom screen, getting anything done that was vaguely meaningful was a joke. For the most part, living in America had become an act, another routine, yet more tap dancing. That was, until it wasn't an act anymore and it became *the thing*.

The challenges of adjusting to life in America, coupled with my own issues, the separation from my family and rising racial tensions had me questioning what I was doing, daily. I was being paid millions, but the buck had to stop somewhere. My health was starting to deteriorate physically, spiritually and mentally. I felt myself unravelling. My better angel was now whispering, 'Bro, it's time to go home.' America, as I realised, might not be my destiny. The allure of the bigger, better deal was gone. I had never curated music with a smash-and-grab mentality, but yes, of course, being a record label exec is about doing deals. And yes, I was about making the record company – and by extension, myself – money, about bigging up what works and burying what doesn't. Ultimately, I was in a results-driven business. You can talk about culture, you can talk about career, you could talk about all those things until you're blue in the face; unless you're delivering results, you never get to any of those things. Results enable you to make all the other things happen. Increasing the trust base increases your power bases, and this enhances your brand, in terms of how people perceive you.

So, you deliver results and you set a high number of what you made for the company one year; so they expect you to make more money the next year, and the next year, and the next year, and they just ratchet it up and up and up. And then COVID hits, and everything stops. Suddenly, all my stuff caught up with me. I'd been running and running and running for so long that nothing could catch up with me because I'd always been on the move.

Over the past couple of years, I'd worked my arse off, under difficult circumstances, but I'd come up short in terms of what I *wanted* to achieve. But personally? Well, I could puff my chest out and say, with immense pride, 'Yeah, I broke America.'

The only downside was, by the same token, America had broken me.

15

Midnight Train to Georgia

He said he's going back to find
What's left of his world
The world he left behind

— Gladys Knight & the Pips[1]

By the time September 2020 came around, it was clear that no one would be returning to the office until at least the New Year. This extended period had me contemplating my next steps, so I reached out to Monte Lipman, who, in the Universal chain of command, was the next senior exec I reported to. I expressed my concerns about being in America during lockdown and the limitations this had imposed on me, personally and professionally, but especially the stress that had been put on my family, with my daughter being unable to travel. As my contract had less than a year left, I suggested taking some time off to go back to the UK, see a doctor and try to resolve things with Darcey.

---

[1] Jim Weatherly; Buddah Records.

'I'm taking two weeks off,' I said. The board seemed non-plussed, like a toddler staring at a Rubik's cube.

'You can't take two weeks off,' they said.

'*I'm taking two weeks off,*' I repeated. I needed a break, otherwise they'd have a broken man on their hands.

I mentioned how my mental health and wellbeing had been shot to pieces in recent months, how it felt like I was basically being denied my constitutional right to 'Life, Liberty and the pursuit of Happiness . . . and two weeks off'.

'No, no, no, no, no . . . Darcus, you take off all the time you need.'

After nearly three years in the Big Apple, I'd come to appreciate that working long hours and weekends is standard, lunch is for wimps and taking more than half a day from the office for medical treatment or a funeral, unless it was for a life-saving procedure or a parent, was frowned upon. Yet here I was, taking *two weeks* off, and it wasn't even Christmas or Easter or Thanksgiving or Halloween. However, no sooner had I stepped off the plane at Heathrow than the daily grind of managers, agents, lawyers and artists were demanding I change, amend, renegotiate or bankroll one thing or the other. While my colleagues and the Universal board had got the 'do not disturb' memo, the rest of the industry hadn't. For them, it was business as usual but in the period that followed, the outpouring of support that I received from my colleagues, family, friends and artists ultimately helped me to heal and restored my faith in the industry that I love. This entire sorry episode taught me that you should never lose sight of the duty of care you owe to your team, colleagues and to your artists.

If you're in this game and committed to discovering and developing authentic talent you better be prepared for the good and the bad and you better be able to do business on their level or on their terms. Many musicians are not accustomed to the bureaucratic bullshit of tax returns, public liability insurance and thirty-day payment terms. Many have managers who are friends and family, who will think nothing of turning up at the office mob-handed if their cheque is late or, God forbid, they have been dropped by the label.

I get that you have to flex for artists, but sometimes you need to know when to draw the line, even if it means losing friends. I've had to turn down or drop black artists only to find them pulling the race card by implying that I 'sold out' simply because they couldn't cut it, creatively or commercially, or because I refused to sign a second-rate artist because I wouldn't be guilt-tripped into giving them a break because of their skin colour. Haters gonna hate, as they say, but I do get where many of these grievances come from. I feel for talented black artists who see mediocre white acts get deals while they languish on the sidelines. Some of this is just down to the nature of the industry, cultural biases and market forces – things I have a limited influence over but have witnessed over the years and continue to see all around me. A lot of what the uninitiated or naïve put down to racism or classism or sexism in the music industry is simply down to what is being offered. Bring me the next Stormzy or Dave and you've got a deal, 100 per cent. But if you come to me with yet another generic grime act babbling on about 'cheffing the mandem' over bootlegged beats off the internet, then all you're going to get from me is tumbleweed.

I've met enough artists over the years to know that creativity often comes at a price. You sign these characters who may have amazing talent but are also so far along the spectrum they've gone off the edge. In fact, I instinctively know how to spot the signs as I grew up in an environment in which everyone seemed to be wrestling with neurodivergent issues, myself included. But, likewise, the corporate world isn't a land of milk, honey and normalcy. I was just part of the machine, part of a system that I feared had only got worse because of the pandemic.

The dehumanising effect that those three 'lost' years had on industries, companies and ordinary people was undeniable. It was as if we'd all been reduced to data and the human connection had been beaten to a pulp. This shift away from humanity was concerning, especially in the creative realm, where you have a subculture of people – regardless of artform or medium – who tend to be highly sensitive, volatile or vulnerable people. I'm not saying that everyone else had a fantastic pandemic and only people in creative industries had a hard time. But if your vocation, your life, your raison d'être is based on a feedback loop that relies on constant physical interaction with people, being treated like a caged animal is no joke.

The essence of the music industry lies in the human connection, the live performances, the gigs, the energy of the crowd and the camaraderie among musicians and fans. It's about the shared experience and the magic that happens when people come together to enjoy music. But when the pandemic hit and everything was forced to go virtual, that sense of connection was lost. The music industry, like many others, had to adapt and find new ways to engage audiences.

That's why, when I reached that point during the lockdown, I realised that this situation was just not sustainable for me, personally or professionally. I missed the thrill of live performances, pressing flesh and the face-to-face interactions with artists, colleagues and fans. The virtual world may have its conveniences, but it simply can't replicate the essence of live music and the sense of community it fosters. The lack of real-life connections and the inability to experience music and art in all its heavenly glory was starting to take its toll on me, those around me and – as endless news reports showed – millions of people around the world.

The looming question, then, was, 'What's next?' What more was there to achieve, especially now that the mortgage had been paid off? That might sound provincial, but remember, my ambitions had been, for the most part, humble; my successes organic. To that extent, lacking the politicking, Machiavellian, chess-playing arch-strategising associated with the leadership classes, some might say I was a CEO without a clue but I like to think of myself as a disruptor, a maverick, a rebel with a cause. And that cause is, and always will be, to quietly, gently, organically shake shit up and not take shit lying down.

Unsurprisingly, the idea of me walking away from Island, Universal and the corporate record industry was met with scepticism by some peers. Conversations with higher-ups at UMG revolved around potential regrets. 'Are you sure you know what you're doing, Darcus?' was the overriding question that was implied, if not occasionally expressed by most of the industry cats I met. Here I was, being viewed by the company, my peers and more and more players within the industry as some sort of prodigal son – the kid who had it all and blew it. I was fine with this. They could think what they liked. I'm not a religious man, but I knew enough about the scriptures to know that when the prodigal son finally comes home, what he finds is redemption.

16

How Can You Mend a Broken Heart

How can you stop the rain from falling down?
Tell me, how can you stop the sun from shining?
What makes the world go 'round?

– Barry and Robin Gibb[1]

Officially, Universal Music Group put out the following statement: 'Darcus informed us of his decision to return to the UK for
personal reasons and to pursue new career opportunities there.
We fully support his decision and we are thankful to Darcus for
his many contributions to Island Records throughout the years.'

Picking up on the statement, entertainment bible *Variety*
reported, 'While the label enjoyed success during Beese's stint
with Shawn Mendes, Demi Lovato and recently signed Sabrina Carpenter, the label did not have a high-profile breakout
and sources say there was unhappiness with its failure to attract

---

[1] Barry Gibb and Robin Gibb; Polydor Records.

hip-hop talent . . . There was no word on a successor at the time of this article's publication.'

And that, as they say, was that. After more than thirty years, I was no longer an employee of Island Records. It was a surreal situation to be in, but looking back, and regardless of the ups and downs of the past few years, I couldn't help but feel grateful for my time at the company. Ultimately, there were a handful of key individuals, including Chris Blackwell, Lucian Grainge and David Joseph, who backed me to prove myself and to go out there and discover and nurture some of the biggest and best artists in the world.

But the clock had finally struck midnight. It was pumpkin time. Me, Alison and Darcus packed up our shit and returned to London, primarily because Darcey was there and she was going through a tough time. On top of everything else that had happened, being apart from her was challenging. Looking back, if I'd had the foresight, I might not have made the move to America in the first place, considering the impact it would have on her. Unfortunately, we can't predict the future and we make the best choices we can with the information we have at the time.

During that lockdown period when Darcey was really struggling, it became clear that some of her past experiences and upbringing were triggering her and bringing her down. This led her to seek therapy. It struck me that my parents had also endured traumatic upbringings and I too had my share of childhood trauma. It seems that in some way, these experiences, distilled and passed down through generations, continue to affect us. It can be quite overwhelming when you realise that even when you're doing your best, it might not feel good enough and the cycle persists, rolling onto the next generation. The sins of the father and all that.

The pandemic had forced me to come up for air that I wasn't ready to breathe at first, but luckily it happened when it happened because if I'd gone another couple of years in America, I would've been properly burnt out. In a way, COVID saved my life. Coming up for air helped me crystallise a lot in terms of my relationship with Alison, Chad, Darcey and Darcus. As much as I thought I'd been present in their lives, I'd short-changed them, and myself. Most of the time I was only there in body, not in mind or soul. I'd become the one thing I swore I'd never be: a cardboard cut-out of a father and a husband.

Going to America and coming back was transformational. I'm still trying to figure out what it all meant, but that three-year period from 2018 to 2021 shaped the course of my life on many levels and in profound ways. I'm not going to say that the chickens came home, but I went to America as one person and came back a different man.

Returning home from the US, it felt like I was standing at a crossroads, both personally and professionally. I needed a reboot. During a conversation with my financial advisor, who has always had my best interests at heart, I had a moment of clarity. We delved deep into what my next move should be and pondered the future. He sensed that I was adrift, lost in a vast sea without something solid to anchor myself to. It was during these moments of reflection, and while writing this book, that the idea of seeking mentorship and guidance emerged as a beacon of hope.

'What is Darcus without Island?' he asked.

I ruminated on that question for a while, then set about finding an answer to it as I realised that I needed to sit with someone who could help me devise and get me in the right rooms with the right people, to co-create the next iteration of Darcus. After all, and here comes the pun we've all been waiting for, no man is an island.

My first port of call was Khoi Tu, a leadership and team-work consultant who has advised the likes of celebrity chef Jamie Oliver, three-time Formula 1 world champion Sir Jackie Stewart and leaders from some of the world's biggest businesses and global politics.

Apart from my parents and a handful of people I've admired in the business space, I'd never felt the need for a mentor in my life until I met Khoi. In the vast and intricate world of business, aside from looking to experts or old heads for advice, there was no one at my level who had helped me navigate a way through my career.

Working at Island for as long as I did, I was never going to be comfortable working for another label. At first, it felt like I'd come out of a thirty-odd-year marriage and what lay ahead were a series of really embarrassing Tinder dates. But that wasn't the case. Having been tapped up by Warner, another one of the 'Big Three', I had a series of conversations with Max Lousada, Warner Music Group's global CEO of Recorded Music, and Tony Harlow, Chairman and CEO of Warner Music UK. Everything Max and Tony said chimed with the direction I wanted to go in: namely, the natural next step for me was to head up my own label while still being part of a broader record company leadership team. I've known Max, Tony and the team for a long time and their commitment to building a community that inspires and supports its artists is very much in line with my own philosophy, so initially I couldn't have been more pleased to be taking this next step with Warner Music and becoming their EVP and president of a new joint-venture label. Being 'back in the mix' with a major label and all the support, structure and status that brought with it, along with access to an incredible talent pool, was not to be sniffed at. But as time went on and I ruminated on how the landscape was changing, I realised that as much as artists were now swerving the major labels to set up shop on their own, record companies also had to respond in kind. The question was, to paraphrase a misquote attributed to Gandhi, *what was the change I wanted to see in the world?* To answer this, inevitably, I had to go it alone.

My vision was to build a new business model, a 360° creative, entertainment and cultural entity, possibly with a Roc Nation vibe to it, which would transcend the top down, by-the-numbers record company system. I wanted to speak to people in a way that was as enlightening as it was entertaining and put music at the heart of the conversation, but without making it the be-all and end-all.

Reflecting on my three decades in the music industry, given all the trials and tribulations, bust-ups and meltdowns, successes and, er, 'unsuccesses', I finally realised that the lyrics, the songs and the artists I'd encountered along the way threaded together a rich tapestry that told a very different story to the one I'd convinced myself – and others had convinced me – was being told. In a way, a breakdown, like a volcanic eruption, is as much an act of creation as it is an act of destruction. People think that creativity is about making stuff. It's not. It's about *changing stuff.* All those years of erupting, exploding and breaking down had run parallel with building, rebuilding, moulding and shaping.

When the time came that I thought I couldn't take anymore, what I was really saying to myself, and those around me, was

I couldn't take any more of *that*. The money, the success, the accolades, the 'breaking America'. . . I'd done it all. I'd grown up in a council house, in a family where there was no such thing as a *side hustle*; life was all about the singular hustle. One hundred per cent. I knew what it meant to be broke and unhappy. But material wealth doesn't guarantee happiness. Mum worked hard to provide for me and despite financial challenges, she found a way to be content. It's a cliché that money doesn't buy you happiness and, generally, I'm not one for hackneyed sayings, ideas and predictable bullshit. But the Bentley, the Hublot and the Manhattan condo never brought me happiness – they were just a way to keep score in a game that's obsessed with status, ostentatiousness and image. It's not called show*business* for nothing.

As I move into this next crucial phase of my career, life, exploration and *being*, I want to bring the wraparound of what I've achieved in the music industry to the cultural fore. I've curated music for the likes of Tate Modern's 'Soul of a Nation' exhibition. I've worked with the Black Curriculum on ways to address Eurocentricity in education. I've sat on countless industry roundtables, such as 'It's OK To Be Black', which aimed to move the dial on race. I've given untold talks, lectures and masterclasses to aspiring artists, entrepreneurs and A&Rs the world over. When I got over myself, when I ignored that gnawing, irrational, you're-not-worth-it imposter syndrome that was linked to childhood trauma and feelings of inadequacy, when I looked at my 'bits', my achievements, my track record, I was like, shit, I did all that. Owning my successes, which perhaps meant also not ignoring my failures, helped to open doors into rooms I once would've thought were off-limits.

In my first session with Khoi, we got to talking about what it is to be a leader, before moving the conversation on to what power looks like and the subtle and intricate ways that people use and leverage it. I couldn't help but think that the archetype of the power player he was describing was Sir Lucian Grainge. I gave Khoi an example of a typical moment with Lucian, which was one of the last times I sat with him before taking up the Island US gig.

'Get a pen and a piece of paper,' Lucian had said. 'Now draw a circle. Great. Now write the word "power".'

'Now *that's* power,' said Khoi.

'Say what?' I asked.

'He got you to draw a circle and write "power". That's power.'

Khoi went on to explain that being a CEO brings with it inherent power, but the nature of that power and how it is wielded varies greatly among individuals. Some choose to use it in a traditional, authoritative manner, while others have a different perspective on power. He suggests that it's not just about holding a position, but about how one uses that position to enact change, to inspire and to lead.

I had experienced success within a major label, but now I wanted something a little more entrepreneurial. I decided that the new collaboration was going to be called 'Darco Recordings'. I felt inspired by the likes of Jay-Z, who have built their empires and have shown that it's possible to be both inside and outside the system, to be top-down and ground-up. The dream was to build something that resonates with the ethos of being black-run, recognising the need for representation and authenticity in leadership and influence, but also Afrocentric in look, feel and, yes, sound. I don't want to be the intermediary anymore. I want people to establish relationships with the music company just as they do with the artist. That's what made my time at Island Records so rewarding: people cared about Island and other brands valued – and envied – that too.

I've always been cautious about individuals who make grandiose claims about their 'vision' before they've actually accomplished anything. It's not uncommon to see these people make a big splash in the media when they launch something only to hear nothing from them a year or two down the line. Thus, I didn't want to be featured in a generic *Music Week* magazine article or *Music Business Weekly* interview feature, bigging myself up and making it all about me instead of focusing on the new venture – regardless of shape or form – and the team behind it.

In this nascent phase, my focus for Darco is creating something with a core identity, a personality and a strength of character that centres our artists, our music and the label's culture – not the executive – at the heart of the operation. In a world in which people discover, consume and fall in love with music in multiple ways, from movie soundtracks to YouTube syncs, shopfloor sound systems to Spotify playlists, from new bands, singers and rappers to digging deep into old school catalogues, I want Darco to make music the message *and* the medium.

In the wake of George Floyd and the impact of the Black Lives Matter movement, there's a lingering sentiment of commitment to diversity and inclusion in the industry. That's obviously a good thing. However, the true test is whether those words can translate into tangible actions.

But what does genuine change look like? Well, for one thing, I want to build diversity and empower people of colour to have entrepreneurial roles within and foster partnerships outside of

Darco and its curatorial landscape with fellow travellers. I want to develop the execs, leaders and agents of change of tomorrow as real power – and real power-sharing – means developing, moulding, shaping and placing people from diverse backgrounds in positions of true influence and not creating symbolic roles with toothless titles and name badges that keep black and brown people endlessly looking up at a glass ceiling as opposed to looking forward to making a difference.

Khoi had really got me going about the nature of true power and to the point where I started to question my own achievements: not self-critically, but in terms of the degree to which patronage played a role in my own success. *No man is an island.* These words resonated with me as I reflected on how the traditional music industry, for all its pizazz, showiness and artistry is fundamentally hierarchical and as such, bestowing someone with the title of 'president' may seem like a significant gesture to anyone on the outside looking in, but within the power structure, it is often more symbolic than substantive.

17

It Dread Inna Inglan

Far noh mattah wat dey say,
Come wat may,
We are here to stay
Inna Inglan
Inna disya time yah . . .

— Linton Kwesi Johnson[1]

While I lived in a world that was far from the streets, and had zero connection to anything or anyone shady, given my background and where I lived, I wasn't immune to the consequences of mindless violence.

Having settled back into nuclear family life in London, one evening Darcey popped round to her boyfriend's place in west London – the very urban village where he'd been born and raised, and a stone's throw away from where I grew up in Fulham. As

---

[1] Linton Kwesi Johnson; Front Line.

the pair were out getting some food at the top of his road, a couple of 'kids' rode up on an electric scooter, snatched his mobile and stabbed him. Thank God, Darcey wasn't seriously injured in the attack and was there to help stem the blood flow from her boyfriend's wounds and race him to hospital where, without exaggerating, they saved his life.

Like a lot of parents, I worry about my kids when they leave the house, when they walk out that front door, when they leave the house and go out into a world you have no control over. Where are they going? What are they doing? I genuinely worry if they'll come back in one piece or come back at all. Now that I'm older, and a little bit wiser, I can see why my mum and dad worried about me when I was growing up. Being a parent is a monumental leap of faith.

What happened to Darcey's boyfriend and the terror it exposed her to was a painful reminder of the nexus between life 'on road' and the kind of music this criminal subculture engenders. This might sound like a bit of a leap, but it doesn't take six degrees of separation to join the dots between the kids spitting about crime and those rolling around on stolen scooters and mopeds committing it. Often, the two are one and the same thing, which can take people like me down a rabbit hole where life imitates art and vice versa – and you're caught in the middle questioning your role in it all.

On a label, as the person who ultimately signs off on the album and its lyrics, the video and its imagery, the marketing campaign and its 'fuck you' messaging, at its edgiest, I'm buying into a subculture in which artists chronicle a daily grind of robbery, violence, drug dealing, drug taking and all-round dysfunctionality. Whether told through rap, drill or grime, there's a global audience out there that can't seem to get enough of this raw, unfiltered, yet highly creative artform. At its best, it's poetic social commentary; but its worst it's just an ad campaign for the kind of fuckers who wouldn't have thought twice about hurting my daughter if she'd got in their way.

Patently, whatever the genre or subgenre, music that comes from the streets, about the streets, is a valid form of expression. But it increasingly puts cultural gatekeepers such as myself in a sticky situation. I'm frequently asking myself: to what extent does music glamorise criminality, gang activity, drug abuse or whatever versus the extent to which it highlights social issues, informs and entertains, gives young people a voice, an outlet and a chance to do something creative in a world where they could be stuck stacking shelves, wasting away on the dole, or worse, selling the drugs and shanking the people they're making records about? Where do we draw the line? Do record labels have a duty of care to the public not to make records about what detractors see as unpalatable material; or should we be free to support our artists in their endeavours, give the audience what they want and reward our shareholders by staying true to the mantra, 'publish and be damned'? At the end of the day, as artists continue to wrestle control away from the major labels and deal directly with their fanbases, and the power of the internet and social media grows bigger and evermore unchecked, is there even anything the mainstream music industry can do about it?

From punk rock to gangsta rap, rock 'n' roll to acid house, the authorities have always stepped on artists' toes and tried to preach to the record industry by scapegoating music, and by extension young people, for society's ills and the failings of politicians. Clearly, both artists and the industry must take responsibility when it comes to the material we put out *and* who is putting it out. In 2020, Wiley was dropped from his management company and investigated by police after posting a series of anti-Semitic tweets.[2] More infamously, Kanye found himself cold-shouldered by record labels, collaborators, sponsors, fans and large swathes of the political and corporate classes for a welter of controversial statements that included anti-Semitic comments, 'White Lives Matter' sloganeering and support for disgraced president Donald Trump.

While people point to mainstream rappers and grime artists such as Jay-Z, 50 Cent, Snoop Dogg, Bugzy Malone or Giggs for infusing their music with lyrics that 'glorify' crime, and more underground outfits actively use their music to promote their own criminal and gang-related activity, I see there being a clear distinction between artists who document past behaviours or illustrate a particular subculture, for creative reasons, and those who use music as a form of criminal talking drums to communicate sick or sadistic messages. For me, the red line is: are you 'at it'? If you are, then I'm not interested. Likewise, as 'authentic' or 'real' or marketable a grime artist might think he or she is, just because they're currently writing their lyrics in a jail cell, I'm not interested.

I'm all for freedom of expression and see censorship, on grounds of taste or morality, as a convenient way of shutting up people whose opinions we'd rather ignore because we don't like what they're reflecting back at us. But it's crucial that this

---

[2] The Metropolitan Police eventually dropped their investigation against Wiley and he was not charged.

fearlessness isn't just blind ambition for the dollar or lacks an understanding of where we come from. There's a sense of fearlessness today, but it often lacks depth. That's why I found it beautiful that Steve McQueen created the 'Small Axe' series of films, one of which, *Mangrove*, paid homage to Mum and Dad's struggle, and used the music of the period to anchor the narrative. (The series title actually comes from a song by the Wailers.) *Mangrove* helped an audience beyond Britain's black community realise that we have a civil rights history right here, in the UK, and it encouraged them to explore it further. Instead of just hearing about incidents like the shooting of Mike Duggan on social media, or watching a riot kick off somewhere with no context, it's vital to dig deeper and understand that these events connect to our past, and that Britain's first generation of West Indian immigrants, the so-called 'Windrush generation' weren't just cheap labour – they were pioneers who changed the face of Britain forever.

Just like my father, connecting to the past, and to the old country, has become increasingly important to me, not just for my own sense of identity but for my children, too. As much as we could, Alison, the kids and myself, used to go and stay with family in Belmont, Trinidad, just as I did as a boy. But if the streets of New York and London had become more and more threatening, in Trinidad they had become untenable for us. The last time we were all there together, we borrowed a guy's car and spent the day just driving around, stopping off at the beach and generally being regular tourists. We brought it back in one piece, but the next day, the guy got shot in a drive-by while sat in that same car. It was a little too close for comfort.

On another visit, on my way back from collecting my uncle from Piarco Airport, my cousin Amoa, now a grown man, received a call on his mobile: it was a warning that there was a hit out on him. I couldn't believe it. We were just about to drive into town in a conspicuous red car with dark tinted windows with my uncle in the back seat and with a price out on my cousin's head. In a country with one of the highest murder rates in the world, this was no joke. I pulled over, the rain lashing down, gave Amoa all the money I had on me and told him to get out of town there and then. He made it out of harm's way on that occasion, but his past caught up with him eventually.

On 20 February 2024, my sister called to tell me that Amoa had been gunned down in a drive-by shooting that morning after dropping his daughter off at school in Belmont. He died just yards from where he had lived, in the old neighbourhood where we'd played as kids, where the future was another country. He was fifty years old.

18

Pride (In the Name of Love)

One man come in the name of love
One man come and go
One man come, he to justify
One man to overthrow

$$- U2^1$$

It was probably the biggest lightbulb moment of my life.

'Mum, I've got something to tell you.'

'What now, Darcus?'

'I've just been diagnosed with ADHD.'

'No, you're not. You're not ADHD.'

The great thing about mums is their endless ability to suspend disbelief about their children, often in the face of expert testimony, irrefutable evidence, or even their own lived experience. I explained that as part of my post-America mental and physical MOT, I had been to see a psychiatrist, did all the tests under

---

[1] U2; Island Records.

the sun, and was diagnosed with ADHD. I even gave her some examples of questions and answers, scenarios and behaviours that were used to form my diagnosis.

'Darcus, what you're describing is *exactly* what I do. Do you think I'm ADHD?'

'Well, he did ask if there was any history,' I said, adding diplomatically, 'The psychiatrist did say that usually at least one of the parents has got it. . . . and I'd probably say, Mum, that you and Dad never really did shoot straight.' I just knew she had it. Suddenly, so much became clearer.

Previously, I never understood why I was able to move on from relationships so easily, whether they be personal or professional. For example, when I knew I was leaving London for New York, I just shut it down and moved on. People asked me, 'Aren't you having a goodbye thing?' and I was like, 'No.' Whether it was being able to move from one friendship group to another, or being able to just drop an act, I could be cold, calculated, cut off and move on.

After all these years, and having had my sneaky suspicions, I was relieved rather than regretful that finally I'd answered an existential question about who the fuck, or what the fuck, I was. Other than OCD, I ticked all the right boxes: social anxiety, attention, blah, blah, blah. While the diagnosis wasn't about to radically change anything about my life, it helped to explain behavioral traits, interests and thought processes that I'd previously just put down to being 'wired differently'. I also like to think it explained my creative bent, given the apparent association between ADHD and creativity. More importantly, though, I hoped this newfound knowledge would help me navigate my relationships with Mum, Alison and the kids with greater sensitivity. Especially if they could now cut me a bit more slack!

While I'd got to the bottom of my mental state, my body was more of a challenge. Obviously, cells can turn cancerous at any time, so I have to monitor my prostate on the regular. Around my fortieth birthday, I felt like my body began to break down. It was like reaching the peak of a roller coaster and then feeling the gut-wrenching descent as your body disintegrates. You never think it's going to happen to you, but you can't cheat the march of time.

Coming out of lockdown and getting back to being more mobile, I came to realise that my shoulders were constantly hunched up. Had I really been walking around like that all this time? Soon, standing became the real issue. I'd be fine stuck in a chair in my office for hours, but within minutes of getting up, a burning sensation would tear through me like a red-hot poker. It then became a challenge to see how long I could bear the pain before needing to sit. Medication would obscure the pain only to make it feel intensified once the drugs wore off. At first, I resisted taking codeine, but eventually I caved. When you look at all the chaos happening in the world, you realise that life is pretty much about managing pain, on a personal, professional or indeed global level. *C'est la vie.*

When I was a kid, I was bouncing off walls without fear every five minutes. As children, the height of a wall or the thrill of an adventure playground swing didn't faze us. We'd effortlessly jump and swing and walk on balcony walls . . . But with age, that same wall seems daunting. As we grow older, our sense of caution heightens. There's a definite need to prepare physically for old age because accidents can be severe. Over time, the shield of invulnerability begins to fade, and you start to think, maybe it's time to bulk up for old age, because I don't want to be falling over with bone on concrete, man!

Since my last scan a year ago, I've lost all the cartilage in my left hip. That's why the pain was so intense. I have an oedema of the bone marrow, floating bone, holes in the femur and no cartilage. My surgeon described it thus: if you had an orange in your hand, and the skin and the pith was the cartilage, peel back the orange, take off the pith and put the orange back in your hand. Now that's your femur in the socket. Because I have a slender frame, I've had to be cautious, especially when it comes to physical activities like running. I need to take extra care, because I'm hypermobile, which can lead to dislocations. My doctor suggested another injection into the synovial fluid to provide some temporary lubrication. But I told him, 'Let's just cut out the cancer and skip to the good part, shall we?'

It was hip replacement time.

The average age for a hip replacement is sixty-five. I was now fifteen years ahead of that. No matter how young you feel mentally, your body has a way of reminding you of the reality of your age. I mean, I still enjoy watching animations and cartoons, and I even collect comics from time to time, and I love sci-fi like a proper geek. But ultimately, there's no escaping the fact that we're born to die, and from the cradle to the grave we're all slowly falling apart, bit by bit.

I often find myself thinking that I'm still young, but when it comes to making decisions in a market that's all about youth and demographics, you have to be realistic. You can't just pretend to be young; you need young people around you for that perspective, otherwise you wind up feeling like a total fake. These days, I value my kids' perspectives more now than ever.

There comes a point where you just have to embrace the fact that you're not the youngest person in the room anymore; you might very well be the oldest. It's a realisation that hits home at times. And when people say things like, 'You're still young for someone in their fifties,' I get what they're saying, but there's an awareness that comes with age.

It's a debate I often have with Alison: no matter how young you think you are, at what point, when you're out clothes shopping, do you say to yourself, 'Can I *really* buy a pair of jeans with rips in them?' You have to stop and ask yourself: can I pass the rip test?

But what really excites me at this age is rediscovering my passion for working in the music industry. Previously, it was all about breaking new artists, but now it's about immersing myself in the world of music once more. When I first started in the job of A&R, it was primarily about finding talent and launching them. However, my initial interest lies not in discovering and breaking artists, but in rekindling my love for the music-making process.

Authenticity is paramount in everything I do. It's essential for people to genuinely believe in and support what Darco is offering. For me, having a hit and achieving success should be a by-product of people believing in my vision. So, my focus lies in how many people I can bring together in a room, rather than just counting the streams a song is receiving right now.

When I chose the name Darco, I didn't want it to be overly clever or catchy. It needed to resonate with culture and hold a sense of authenticity. It's partly as a homage to Dad, partly because I love the name Darcus and wanted to have that signature, that familial heritage woven into the brand. What I didn't want was a brand or an image like one of those classic Westerns – you know, the ones with the make-believe town they're trying to persuade you is real. I wanted to avoid becoming a façade where the front looks substantial, but when you look closely and peek behind, it's made of plywood and propped up by cheap wooden supports.

Music holds a fascinating place in culture; it intersects with almost everything. Music becomes the soundtrack of life, you know? It can complement and enhance most experiences. What continues to fascinate and excite me is when people ask me what the best thing is about having a hit. It's knowing that the song touched someone's life at a significant moment for them. It's very simple, really: it's about soundtracking people's lives.

I've always believed that success is like a garden, and it's often sown in the garden of failure. It's why I've always allowed those around me the time and space to experience setbacks because that's how I came up. Even today, as a grown individual, I still look back and wonder if I could have done things differently. The answer is yes, I could have. So, instead, you give yourself and others the room to grow. Whether you're an artist or an executive, your craft is about nurturing the creative process, even amid challenges. It's a skill you develop over the years, understanding how things work, from the inception of a song to the final product delivery, and continually evolving that understanding. Artists' development and personal growth never cease. Early on, success was about quantifiable achievements like chart positions or sold-out venues. But as you age and gain more experience, you realise that real success is about having a lasting career. It's not just about one-hit wonders or brief flashes of success. It's about being here thirty, maybe forty or even fifty years later, regardless of the ups and downs. That's what defines true success.

I salute everyone who's been on this ride with me, including those whose wheels fell off along the way. My body might not be what it used to be, no one's is, but that doesn't stop me from growing. For me, there's always another bullet in the chamber, another opportunity to explore.

Reinvention and regeneration are critical to an ever-evolving industry like the music business. But it's not easy to reinvent yourself without coming across as if you're doing it just for the sake of it, merely trying to stay relevant. Anyone can put on a big floppy hat and a pink tartan suit and say they've 'reinvented' themselves. Madonna, for instance, was adept at commercialising and reinventing herself during the first two decades of her career. She managed to mirror the current trends, adapt, and remain on the cutting edge, staying relevant. But in more recent times she has become a parody of her own reinventive self.

Just as back catalogue has a reinventive quality in the way it introduces new audiences to classic material, history has the same effect. History is the back catalogue of life. I like that. Since a wider audience has come to know who my mum and dad are because of Steve McQueen's *Mangrove Nine* film, they now join up the dots when they meet me and say, 'And they had you, and you've done this and that? Wow!' That makes me part of living history. I'd be a liar if I said I didn't have the occasional 'holy shit' moment, pinch myself, and accept that for all my personal and professional achievement, I *am* a small cog in a big wheel, but that wheel isn't corporate hamsters; it's part of a tradition, a struggle, a movement that's as relevant today as it was when Mum and Dad were on the streets fighting for black people's civil rights, and the generations that came before them going back decades and decades.

As a legacy, this probably doesn't make it easy for Darcey, my daughter, as she follows in my footsteps and starts to chart her own path in the music industry, with just a little bit of help from her old man. There's a weight of expectation on her shoulders, just as there was on mine. Likewise, as my son Darcus carries my name and my father's name forward, maybe he'll find there's baggage that comes with a familial and cultural association, too. Hopefully, he'll also find it serves as a calling, every now and again.

I'm the first to admit that many of the hits I've had were, when viewed through a hyper-critical lens, very superficial, like fast food for the emotions. The world has already forgotten about that stuff. That's pop music for ya. But there are a few evergreen songs, like Amy Winehouse's 'Love is a Losing Game', that will endure the test of time, and when you brush away the dust of time, you will see that 'Darcus woz 'ere'.

Like many people – highly driven, successful or even who never fully realise their ambitions – in the background there's always been a desire to earn my parents' respect, live up to their expectations. Some people rail against their parents' values or beliefs and actively carve out a niche for themselves that's 'not a chip off the old block'. But for me, like Barbara Beese and Darcus Howe, I've always been driven by what I'm prepared to stand, fight and die on a hill for. I hate injustice, I can't stand people taking the piss, and I will take liberty-takers to task. Maybe it's about trying to please my parents. Maybe it's about proving that that radical DNA runs through me, too. Whatever. I *am* my parents' son.

So, I'm keeping up the family tradition, but I'm doing it in a different way. I wouldn't say I've got an agenda as that sounds loaded. All I'm trying to do with the odd pop song here and there is use my influence, my expertise, my know-how and, yes, my idea of what's fucking cool, to give the voices we need to hear the platforms they need to jump on and spread the message. If I can do that, and in some way effect some sort of social change by chipping away at the edges of things, then I'm golden. Music, like painting, filmmaking and literature, is such a powerful art form, such a powerful medium, such a powerful way to get into people's heads and touch their hearts. For me, I guess it was never really about selling records. It was about selling a message. I'm still that skinny lickle kid in a vest and raggedy flares, demonstrating, protesting, shouting and screaming, standing on the shoulders of giants with a placard, and fighting the power.

One hundred per cent.

Soundtrack to My Years

Taio Cruz – 'Dynamite'

Sugababes – 'Round Round'

Amy Winehouse – 'Rehab – Remix'

Robyn – 'Dancing on My Own'

John Newman – 'Love Me Again'

Hozier – 'Take Me to Church'

Gabriella Cilmi – 'Sweet About Me'

Mutya Buena – 'Real Girl'

Amy Winehouse – 'Our Day Will Come'

Giggs – 'Peligr'o

Remi Wolf – 'Photo ID'

Shawn Mendes – 'Monster (Shawn Mendes & Justin Bieber)'

U2 – 'Get Out of Your Own Way'

Robbie Williams – 'Candy'

Dizzee Rascal – 'Bassline Junkie'

Rizzle Kicks – 'Mama Do the Hump'

Annie Lennox – 'Angels from the Realms of Glory'

JP Cooper – 'September Song'

Big Shaq – 'Man's Not Hot'

Tinchy Stryder – 'Number 1'

Mumford & Sons – 'I Will Wait'

Ben Howard – 'Keep Your Head Up'

Catfish and the Bottlemen – 'Cocoon'

Florence and the Machine – 'You've Got the Love'

Emotional Oranges – 'West Coast Love'

Bombay Bicycle Club – 'Always Like This'

George The Poet – '1,2,1,2'

Devlin – '(All Along the) Watchtower – Radio Edit'

MC Fioti – 'Bum Bum Tam Tam'

Wiley – 'Take That – Edit'

Keane – 'Spiralling'

PJ Harvey – 'The Words that Maketh Murder'

Marshmello – 'OK Not to Be OK'

Skip Marley – 'Slow Down'

Buju Banton – 'Lamb of God'

V V Brown – 'Shark in the Water'

Scarlxrd – 'HELL IS XN EARTH'

Dermot Kennedy – 'Glory'

RAY BLK – 'Run Run'

Angel – 'Wonderful'

Toni Braxton – 'Do it'

Disclosure – 'Latch'

Jessie Reyez – 'IMPORTED (with 6LACK)'

Jessie Ware – 'Wildest Moments'

KSI – 'Goes Off'

Oh Wonder – 'Ultralife'

Alex Clare – 'Too Close'

Clock Opera – 'Lesson No. 7'

DJ Snake – 'You Know You Like it'

The Fisherman's Friends – 'Haul Away Joe'

Jack Garratt – 'Worry

James Morrison – 'I Won't Let You Go'

Paul Weller – '22 Dreams'

Dappy – 'Rockstar'

Bon Jovi – 'Do What You Can'

Sabrina Carpenter – 'Skin'

Josh Osho – 'Redemption Days

Will Young – 'Joy'

The Specials – '10 Commandments'

Sigrid – 'Don't Kill My Vibe'

Baby Rose – 'Borderline'

Tulisa – 'Young – Radio Edit'

Lady Sovereign – 'Hoodie – Mizz Beats Remix featuring Skepta,
JME, Jammer, Ears and Baby Blue'

Dionne Bromfield – 'Mama Said'

Stare – 'Stare'

The Killers – 'Blowback'

joe unknown – 'WISH I AINT'

Rizzle Kicks – 'Down with the Trumpets'

Sugababes – 'About You Now'

keshi – 'LIMBO'

Wookie – 'Scrappy'

RLY – 'Superpower

Jessie J – 'Do it Like a Dude'

Tom Jones – 'Burning Hell'

Emotional Oranges – 'Personal'

Me One – 'La La Hey (Revisited)'

Sean Paul – 'No Lie'

Will Young – 'Love Revolution'

Jessie J – 'Price Tag'

Rockers Hi-Fi – 'Push Push – Original Mix'

Jonathan Jeremiah – 'See (It Doesn't Bother Me)'

MONA – 'Shooting the Moon'

Cleo Sol – 'Never the Right Time (Who Do You Love)'

Florence and the Machine – 'Ship to Wreck'

Sugababes – 'About You Now'

Bombay Bicycle Club – 'Lights Out, Words Gone'

McFly – 'iF U C Kate'

Sean Paul, J Balvin – 'Contra La Pared'

M.I.A. – 'K.T.P. (Keep the Peace)'

To listen to the *Rebel With a Cause* playlist, scan this code in the Spotify app:

Acknowledgements

I offer my thanks, appreciation and respect to all those afore-mentioned artists, colleagues, collaborators, facilitators, friends and global family who have inspired me from the very beginning. Without you, there would be no rebel, no cause, and no book worth writing, or indeed reading. To this end, I need to give special thanks to Chris Blackwell, Lucian Grainge, David Joseph, Monte and Avery Lipman and Michelle Anthony. To those I have not mentioned in these pages, you know who you are. Your names have either been expunged to protect the innocent or gloss over the guilty! Needless to say, this book was never meant to be a kiss-and-tell tale, so thank you to all those unsung heroes (and villains) who have graced me with their confidences, trust and intimacies, and have shown me that discretion truly is the better part of valour.

I'd like to express my gratitude to David Matthews, who gave a voice to my thoughts, feelings, idiosyncrasies and recollections without breaking a sweat. Thank you to Pete Selby and the team at Nine Eight Books for their encouragement, understanding and patience and to David Olusegun for convincing me that the time was right to put pen to paper.

But most of all, I want to thank my wife, Alison, who has been with me through the sunshine and light but also in dungeons dark and grim; my children, Darcey, Darcus Jr and Chad, for putting up with me; The Tribe: Tamara, Taipha, Rap, Claire, Amiri and Zoe; and my mother and father, Barbara Beese and Darcus Howe, for pointing me in a direction of travel I'll never turn back on.